Clematis

as Companion Plants

Clematis

as Companion Plants

B ARRY F RETWELL

CASSELL

To my wife, whose creative colour schemes have inspired most of the photography in this book.

Cassell Publishers Limited
Villiers House, 41/47 Strand
London WC2N 5JE

Text and photographs copyright © Barry Fretwell 1994

First published 1994

British Library Cataloguing in Publication Data
A catalogue record for this book is available from the British Library

ISBN 0-304-34424-9

Distributed in the United States by
Sterling Publishing Co., Inc.,
387 Park Avenue South, New York, NY 10016–8810

Distributed in Australia by
Capricorn Link (Australia) Pty Ltd
PO Box 665, Lane Cove, NSW 2066

Typeset by Litho Link Ltd, Welshpool, Powys, Wales

Printed and bound in Slovenia

HALF TITLE PAGE
C. 'Pink Fantasy'/C. 'Haku Ookan'

TITLE PAGE
C. 'Lady Betty Balfour'/*Lonicera periclymenum*

Contents

Introduction

ALLIED TO A tremendous surge of interest in clematis during recent years, there has developed a far greater knowledge and appreciation of the range and diversity offered by this genus and the glories that it can bestow upon any garden. It is not surprising, therefore, that a number of growers are realizing the potential of combining clematis, not only with other clematis but with, through and in proximity to already existing shrubs and trees.

The following text does assume some acquaintance with clematis; if, however, from the photographs within these pages your interest is stimulated for the first time, a number of books have been published recently from which you can glean a basic knowledge. The main requirement for growing clematis as companion plants is to regard your garden as a canvas and, if not talented with brush and paint – but envious of that gift – allow your spade and trowel to be substitute tools.

Choice of plants is individual, and discipline in the art comes from the need to consider differing growth habits, heights and pruning needs in order to achieve the results envisaged. A guide to these points is given in the following chapters. It is in no way a precise art – Mother Nature's vagaries deem that it shall not be, particularly with her seasons, of late, doing much to frustrate the gardening fraternity.

The winter months may seem ideal for planning and dreaming, and indeed they are, for those gardeners blessed with a retentive memory. The majority, though, may find it easier to make use of a break in summer gardening and roughly map and note trees, shrubs and other features that are intended to host or neighbour the intended clematis. A few photographs will be of tremendous help in capturing the all-important colourings and textures. Given the years of increasing splendour that can be expected, a little summer-time study is worthwhile in order to achieve your objective.

If you are considering companion planting, your garden setting is probably at a reasonable stage of development and the initial hard work accomplished; therefore, the exercise should be one of anticipation and enjoyment – so indulge and be adventurous!

C. macropetala 'Snowbird'/*Taxus baccata* 'Fastigiata'
My first introduction, shown in climbing mode, its pristine beauty
outlined against a yew.

Cultivation

ABOVE
C. 'Burma Star'/*Choisya ternata*

BACKGROUND
C. *alpina* 'Jacqueline du Pré'/*Ceanothus prostratus*

HERE ARE CERTAIN cultural requirements which apply to clematis generally, no matter in which position they are grown. They prefer soil which is moisture-retentive but free-draining. Dry, sandy soils are not liked but it is possible, with the addition of humus and particular attention to watering, to grow clematis to the extent of achieving a reasonable show – if not spectacularly well! This is not so, however, on heavy, wet, cold soils, and clematis rarely do well in these conditions. Before coming to the actual planting, consideration of the best type of plant to look for is worth noting here. It should, of course, look healthy, with dark green foliage – not sickly yellow as sometimes offered. (When purchasing in the autumn, however, allowance must be made for the natural colouring of ageing.) A large-sized container does not mean that a better plant is being acquired or that a better show will be achieved in a shorter space of time. Plants in a 4½ in (11 cm) deep pot, 2–3 ft (60–90 cm) tall, with roots just showing from the bottom of the pot, should be at the ideal stage for planting out.

If you are gardening on a light, free-draining soil, autumn is the best time for planting clematis, but on heavier soils it is probably wiser to wait until the spring – although planting is permissible right through the year, of course, as they are transplanted from pots. Whichever time the clematis are planted, keeping them well watered for the first season is of paramount importance. Always try to give your clematis a good start, remembering that a home is being made for a plant that will provide an almost continuous display for many years.

Remove about a cubic foot (0.03m³) of soil and mix with it a generous amount of well-rotted compost or peat and, unless already gritty, a small amount of sharp sand or grit. Into the bottom of the hole place a 2 in (5 cm) layer of well-rotted garden compost or farmyard manure. Not everyone has access to these, but peat or one of the bagged humus materials available from garden centres can be used as an alternative. Replace 2 in (5 cm) of the removed soil on top and dust with a generous handful of bonemeal. Remove the plant from its container and place in the hole with the original pot level 2–3 in (5–7 cm) below soil level. This deep planting is a guarantee that, in the event of damage or wilt, there will be basal buds able to shoot again.

If the plant is to be trained along or over a fence, pergola or archway, the planting hole can be close to the base, but on a house wall – where the soil is invariably bone dry – try to plant at least 12 in (30 cm) away from it. The long, string-like roots of the large-flowered hybrids and the *viticella* group will probably be wound around the bottom of the pot; these can be carefully teased out and spread along the bottom of the hole. The fine, thread-like roots of most species and small-flowered hybrids should not be disturbed in any way, even if they appear to be pot-bound. After replacing the soil, lightly fork in a handful of a general fertilizer such as blood, fish and bone or John Innes base fertilizer. Give the plant a good soaking and, while still moist, top dress within an 18 in (45 cm) circle with well-rotted manure, compost, peat or chipped bark to a depth of 2–3 in (5–7 cm).

C. viticella 'Elvan'/*Viburnum opulus* 'Xanthocarpum'
Berries are the match, in this instance, for the versatile *C. viticella* 'Elvan'.

Clematis prefer a rich soil and a moist, cool root-run – and this feed and mulch method is the best way of achieving this. There is, however, one drawback in that blackbirds delight in scattering this carefully placed mulch far and wide (usually over paths and patios). If a lot of trouble is experienced in this respect, the answer is to place either slabs or flat stones on top of the mulch. I prefer to plant low-growing plants around the base of the clematis in order to provide the necessary shade; although not quite as effective at stopping the 'scattering' nuisance, it is far more attractive.

Clematis are not self-clinging; they climb by wrapping their leaf-stalks around any suitable host. It follows, therefore, that some form of support must be provided. Against stone, brick or a wooden fence, thin galvanized wire stretched between vine eyes in 12 in (30 cm) squares is hard to better. On walls which need to be painted, wooden trellis panels can be screwed to small blocks, allowing the whole plant and trellis to be bent over while any necessary decorating is carried out. Whichever kind of support is used, try to tie in the new growth to cover the whole area, as, left to their own devices, clematis have an immense desire to rush straight for the top in one tangled rope.

C. montana 'Peveril'/*Lychnis coronaria*
This clematis is able to counter such a contrasting frontispiece – without giving ground!

OPPOSITE
C. viticella 'Etoile Violette'/*Rosa* 'Golden Showers'
The vibrancy of the rose does wonders for this clematis by highlighting the stamens.

The aim of this book is to show how clematis can be better integrated into the garden, and there are certain cultural variations to observe if they are to be used successfully as companion plants. A number of writers in horticultural books and magazines have recently extolled the virtues of growing clematis through trees and shrubs – obviously without personal experience of doing so! I know, from a large number of inquiries, that many gardeners have experienced failure with this, simply by choosing clematis that are totally unsuitable for the chosen position. Herein lies the key to success, for clematis and host must be matched carefully for combination planting. An instruction to avoid planting a *C. montana* or other strong grower on a small tree or shrub may seem superfluous but it is surprising how often it is done. The most common cause of failure, however, seems to stem from the other

extreme, that of trying to train a short-growing hybrid into a large tree. The majority of trees and shrubs will host a clematis of some kind, but really greedy trees like sycamore, large cherries, ash and willow are best forgotten. More details regarding host plants are given in the following pages.

The above notes on planting also apply when combining clematis with trees and shrubs, but with some extra observations. Try to plant on the north, or more shady, side of the host plant, although this counsel of perfection will be dictated by the space between the roots. I have always found rather strange the usual recommendation of planting into the outer extremities of a tree by means of a pole or rope. This natural drip line is where the tree's main feeding roots are concentrated, and it also leaves a permanently vulnerable stem open to physical damage when working in the garden. If the shrub to be used is large, or particularly dense, then plant the clematis on the outer edge and lead it into the branches rather than under the canopy, where a young plant will have difficulty reaching daylight. Small shrubs, prostrate or open branched ones such as magnolias, present no problem and even short-growing clematis may be planted quite close.

It seems to be taken for granted that when a rose is planted it must be regularly fed and cosseted, yet few gardeners consider the need to give the same treatment to their clematis. Clematis are gross feeders, and in return for a small amount of effort they will amply repay you with a sumptuous display year after year. Each February or March, lightly fork into the soil around each plant one good handful of John Innes base fertilizer or blood, fish and bone. Mulch with a 2 in (5 cm) layer of well-rotted compost or peat; mushroom compost is ideal and readily available. In June, give another handful of dry fertilizer or, alternatively, apply a liquid feed every three weeks throughout the growing season. Keep well watered during the first year after planting; this is even more important when the clematis is having to compete with the tree or shrub which is acting as its host.

C. viticella 'Mme Julia Correvon'/apple tree
This generous clematis is seen doing what it does best – hugging a trunk!

Pruning

ABOVE
C. 'Peveril Pearl'/Corylus maxima 'Purpurea'

BACKGROUND
C. macropetala 'Markham's Pink/*Prunus laurocerasus*

*A*CLEMATIS IS USUALLY purchased with the idea in mind of covering some large area as quickly as possible, so the very idea of cutting back this small bundle of twigs which has just been planted seems to verge on the sacrilegious. The normal response to uncertainty is to leave well alone and see what transpires – which is all too evident when one sees the many 'sad', overgrown specimens looking forlorn when they were meant to adorn.

Certainly, if no pruning were to be carried out at all, the plants would still grow and flower reasonably well, though not always in the chosen position. They would either be somewhere high out of sight or in a huge, matted mass, blocking path or doorway. There must be a degree of order if an article on pruning is to be helpful,

C. texensis 'Sir Trevor Lawrence'/
Berberis darwinii
Texensis as grown through a shrub: the glow of 'Sir Trevor Lawrence' vies with the glossiness of the berberis.

OPPOSITE
C. texensis 'The Princess of Wales'/
Rosa 'Blanche Double de Coubert'
The versatility of this outstanding cultivar is illustrated as it scrambles through a shrub rose in an open garden situation.

but if the reader follows instructions slavishly without exercising common sense and observation, and if all plants receive identical treatment, it follows that some will prosper better than others.

To get the best from your clematis, it is necessary to take into account the way in which different varieties grow. Some have stiff, upright growth, others have spreading, slender stems; some are weakly, others more vigorous. The whole subject is full of perplexities, perpetuated by the many different and unnecessarily complicated methods which have been advocated. For pruning purposes, clematis are usually divided into three categories which are referred to in the following descriptions as Groups A, B, and C. As the aim of this book is to extend planting away from the usual walls and fences, the variations on pruning for these methods are described accordingly.

GROUP A

Apart from a couple of early evergreens, the clematis in this category bloom in the spring from April to May, the flowers being produced from dormant buds in the leaf axils of the previous season's growth. It follows, therefore, that any growth removed between late autumn and early spring will result in that amount of flower being lost. Representative of this group are the justifiably popular *C. macropetala* and *C. montana*.

There are thousands of examples of *C. montana* which have never seen secateurs or pruning knife and which, every spring, produce the most incredible waterfalls of bloom. If these are growing into and over a large tree (*C. montana* and *C. vitalba* being the only ones capable of doing this), there is nothing that can be, or needs to be, done about pruning. However, where they are planted for the purpose of quick coverage in a small area, or are merely outgrowing their allotted space, it soon becomes apparent that some form of restraint is needed if this exuberance is to be curbed. *C. montana*, its close relatives and *C. armandii* annually throw out pencil-thick trails many yards long – and even first-time pruners, who would shirk cutting through the thin-stemmed hybrids, will quite happily attack these.

A greater challenge is faced with the *C. alpina* and *C. macropetala* varieties, whose slender, wiry stems grow into an entangled mass, defying detection as to where the shoots start and end. All in this group (even the evergreen *C. armandii*, which, according to many pundits, dislikes being pruned) can be cut back severely as soon as possible after flowering, preferably no later than the end of July, thus giving time for new growth to ripen for next season's flowers. It is better to prune every year rather than wait until the plant becomes overwhelming, as no clematis likes being cut back into the really old trunk – often showing this in the ultimate way!

C. alpina and *C. macropetala*, when established on a vertical, flat surface, are most easily pruned by trimming back to about 6 in (15 cm) from the wall face with a pair of shears. This method is also appropriate to a *C. montana* which has been tied in to cover a given area, and also to trim back the secondary growth which occurs after the initial pruning. When planted in combination with other plants, the primary concern with this group is that of the clematis overpowering its partner rather than vice-versa. The *C. montana* group are best planted on medium- to large-sized trees, choosing a correspondingly vigorous variety of *C. montana* to the ultimate size of the tree, and thereafter left to their own devices. The *C. alpina* types are better accommodated on medium- to large-sized

C. koreana var. *lutea/Rhododendron scintilans*
This dainty clematis nestles in a suitably sized and coloured host.

shrubs and may need more drastic pruning than when grown as a solitary specimen. Do not be afraid to cut out a large proportion of a strong-growing clematis; a far more pleasing effect is achieved if the flowers are diffused lightly over a shrub rather than settled in a congested mass on one side only.

Some of the more tender evergreens, such as *C. cirrhosa*, *C. indivisa* and *C. afoliata*, will in all probability receive a natural pruning during our winters; removing all dead growth around about April will usually suffice.

GROUP B

This is the largest group numerically, covering all the most commonly grown mid-season hybrids, and is sometimes further sub-divided into two sections. First there are the large-flowered hybrids which flower *en masse* in May and June, on short growths with one or two pairs of leaves, terminating in a single flower – usually with a lighter crop of smaller flowers in the autumn. These

C. 'Lady Caroline Nevill'/*Rosa* 'Crépuscule'
Elegant beauty, well matched.

are exemplified by varieties such as the well-known C. 'Nelly Moser', C. 'Vyvyan Pennell' and C. 'James Mason'. The second sub-section is typified by varieties such as C. 'Lawsoniana' and C. W.E. Gladstone'. They normally produce fewer flowers at any one time than the first sub-section but make up for this by their superior size. The main flowering is normally two to three weeks later and produced on longer laterals; thereafter, flowering is intermittent on new growth right through until the autumn. Some of these are rather tall, straggly growers and ideal for climbing among tall wall shrubs and climbing roses. As all the clematis in this group require the same pruning treatment, it does not matter if the name of a particular plant is not known – one which may well have been inherited with the property, perhaps. A long-neglected plant of this group can be brought back to life by cutting away all the tangled top growth until some kind of recognizable framework can be seen; this can then be trained and tied in as for a young plant.

With a newly purchased plant, the main requirement is to try to form a semi-permanent framework. After planting, cut the stem right back to about 12 in (30 cm) above ground level. The ensuing shoots that arise should then be taken horizontally to the left and right of the main stem; this method will produce far more shoots to train up the wall than the 'pinching out of the tips' method usually advised. The rapidity with which new shoots grow away never fails to amaze me and, if the stems are not separated and tied in, they shoot skywards in one great rope and the whole exercise becomes a waste of time.

From the second year onwards, cut out all dead wood and any very spindly shoots during February and March. The rest of the stems should be cut back to the topmost pair of large, fat green buds – which may be anything from a few inches to 1–2 ft (30–60 cm) from the tips of last year's growth. Snip as many of these shoots free from their support as time and patience will allow, then spread them out and re-tie them so as to cover and ultimately flower over as large an area as possible. Clematis in this group require no different treatment if grown in the open garden, but again the most common cause of failure is choosing a companion with too vigorous a constitution – or trying to combine a modest grower with an uncompromising host.

C. 'Kathleen Wheeler'/C. 'Veronica's Choice'
Two large-flowered hybrids: a contrast of shape and compatibility in colouring.

C. 'Peveril Peach'/*Eucalyptus gunnii*
A light and lyrical composition, as befits such a dainty new introduction.

Group C

This group contains all those clematis which need to be pruned more severely than any of the others and, by the very practicability of this, is therefore the easiest to deal with. All too often, one sees *C. × jackmanii*, or similar, swaying disconsolately in the breeze like a dried corpse on a gallows, its large, tangled mass of 'hair' held high in the air over 8–10 ft (2.4–3 m) of lanky brown body. Any clematis that carries all its blooms on the current season's growth and which normally has a flowering period between late June and October will fall into this category, examples being *C. × jackmanii*, *C. viticella* and *C. flammula*. Most (although no hard and fast rules can be given) grow tall, making between 10 and 20 ft (3–6 m) of growth in a season. In the case of the *viticella* and × *jackmanii* types – and some of the species – the flowers occur on the final few feet of new growth. As the majority of these recommence new growth in the spring, at or near the point of cessation from the previous year, it is obvious that they will soon grow out of sight or into a tangled mass if nothing is done to curtail them. With clematis grown on walls or pergolas, simply cut through the entire bundle of stems at a distance of 12–15 in (30–40 cm) above ground level during late February or March. Pull away all of last year's old growth and do not worry about the big, green, healthy-looking buds or shoots that have to be cut away – they will soon be replaced!

Many of the clematis in this group are eminently suitable for growing through trees and shrubs; indeed, they look far better that way. If the intention is to grow them in this manner, then slight modifications to the pruning method will be called for. If grown on a shrub or small tree where the height of the host is more likely to equal that of the climber, hard pruning, as recommended for wall-trained plants, should suffice. If growing through a tree which is taller than the clematis, try cutting back last year's growth to a point about head height; but if the resultant growth does not reach the required height, the only option is to leave well alone and allow the clematis to make its own way into the light. The pruning method used when clematis are to grow through trees is not a precise art, as so many secondary factors come into play, so trial and error – plus a little common sense – will be needed.

There are a few clematis that, for ease, are slotted into this group but which in practice sit rather uncomfortably astride the B and C fence. Examples of these include *C.* 'Mrs Cholmondeley', *C.* 'Hagley Hybrid' and *C.* 'Niobe'. If treated as for Group C and cut hard back, the easiest choice, they will flower very well on their young growth in late summer and autumn. However, if pruned less

C. 'Arabella'/*Buddleia davidii* 'Royal Red'
The rich colouring of the buddleia emphasizes the stripes on the sepals
of 'Arabella'.

severely as instructed for Group B, they will start to flower in May
with even larger flowers, and with the added virtue of flowering
spasmodically right through until autumn. The disadvantage is that
they continue to throw long shoots from near the ends of the
previous year's growth, the flowers and leaves growing ever further
away, with the bottom few feet of naked vine following closely
behind. One method is to cut them hard back one year and prune
lightly the following year; another, once they are large enough, is
to treat each plant as two separate halves – and cut each half hard
back in alternate years.

THE THREE PRUNING GROUPS	
Group A	
C. afoliata	*C. japonica*
C. alpina (all)	*C. koreana*
C. armandii	*C. koreana* var. *lutea*
C. chrysocoma	*C. macropetala* (all)
C. columbiana	*C. montana* (all)
C. fasciculiflora	*C. ochotensis*
C. forsteri	*C. tosaensis*
C. gentianoides	*C. verticillaris*
C. indivisa	
Group B	
'Barbara Dibley'	'Lady Northcliffe'
'Beauty of Worcester'	'Lasurstern'
'Bees Jubilee'	'Lord Nevill'
'Belle Nantaise'	'Louise Rowe'
'Burma Star'	'Miss Bateman'
'Chalcedony'	'Moonlight'
'Countess of Lovelace'	'Mrs Cholmondeley'
'Daniel Deronda'	'Mrs P.B. Truax'
'Dawn'	'Mrs Spencer Castle'
'Dr Ruppel'	'Nelly Moser'
'Duchess of Edinburgh'	'Patricia Ann Fretwell'
'Elsa Späth'	'Peveril Pearl'
C. florida 'Alba Plena'	'Proteus'
C. florida 'Sieboldii'	'Scartho Gem'
'Haku Ookan'	'The President'
'H.F. Young'	'Veronica's Choice'
'Kathleen Wheeler'	'Vyvyan Pennell'
'Kiri Te Kanawa'	'W.E. Gladstone'
'Lady Caroline Nevill'	'William Kennett'
Group C	
C. aethusifolia	'Cascade'
C. akebioides	*C. coactalis*
C. apiifolia	'Comtesse de Bouchaud'
'Arabella'	*C. connata*
C. × *aromatica*	*C.* × *durandii*
'Ascotiensis'	'Edward Pritchard'
C. campaniflora	*C.* × *eriostemon* 'Heather Herschell'
'Caroline'	*C.* × *eriostemon* 'Hendersonii'

Group C continued	
C. fargesii var. *soulei*	'Peveril Peach'
C. fusca	'Peveril Pendant'
'Gipsy Queen'	*C. pierrottii*
C. heracleifolia var. *davidiana*	'Prince Charles'
C. heracleifolia 'Wyevale'	*C. recta* 'Peveril'
C. × 'Huldine'	*C. recta* 'Purpurea'
C. integrifolia (all)	'Rhapsody'
C. × *jackmanii* 'Alba'	*C. serratifolia*
C. × *jackmanii* 'Superba'	*C. stans*
'John Huxtable'	'Star of India'
C. × *jouiniana* 'Praecox'	*C. tangutica*
'Lady Betty Balfour'	*C. terniflora*
C. lasiandra	*C. texensis* (all)
'Lord Herschell'	*C. thibetana*
'Mme Baron Veillard'	*C.* × *triternata* 'Rubro-marginata'
'Mme Edouard André'	'Victoria'
C. orientalis (all)	*C. viorna*
'Pagoda'	*C. viticella* (all)
'Perle d'Azur'	

Group B/C	
'Hagley Hybrid'	*'Niobe'*
'Maureen'	*'Pink Fantasy'*

C. terniflora/Sorbus aucuparia
The clematis is one of the last on
the scene, late enough to
accompany the berries of
the sorbus.

Diseases
and Pests

ABOVE
C. akebioides/Lonicera nitida

BACKGROUND
C. armandii/Alnus glutinosa

*I*N COMPARISON TO many popular garden plants, clematis suffer far less from serious disease and pest attack. However, the one major disease that can be encountered – clematis wilt – is a serious and frustrating problem. This fungal infection has been the cause of much anguish and disappointment for clematis growers for well over 100 years and, sad to say, we are not a great deal closer to solving the problem. Although two fungi have been identified as the probable causes of wilt, this only allows us to live with the disease, as no certain cure is yet available.

Another unexplained perplexity is why it is mainly the large-flowered hybrids that are affected; it is rarely a problem among the small-flowered hybrids, and I have never known any of the species to be troubled by it. *Clematis armandii* and related evergreens, however, are sometimes attacked by *Ascochyta*, which causes leaf spots and encircles the nodes, causing die-back above the infected point, but the disease is not severe enough to trouble these strong-growing species unduly.

Clematis wilt can occur at any stage of growth and one, or all, of the stems may be affected. The most usual time of attack, however, is when, after watching the swelling flower buds in eager anticipation of them opening during the next day or two, suddenly – as if cut through with a knife – the plant hangs limply, leaves as well as flower buds, and over the next few days the whole plant gradually changes to dark brown. If we knew the mode of attack by the fungi we would, at least, have a starting point for a cure; as it is, we can only work within the confines of the scant knowledge available. In practical terms, this means treating the plants before the attack occurs, as nothing can revive a plant once the symptoms have been noticed. Watering the base of the plant with a solution of benomyl at ¼ oz to 3 gallons (7 gm to 14 litres) every three weeks through the growing season has given promising results, and, although it cannot be guaranteed to eliminate wilt altogether, it will ensure that a major proportion of your clematis survives. Once a plant has wilted, cut away all the dead top growth down to ground level and await the appearance of new shoots from below ground level. Reappear they will, for no matter how frustrating clematis wilt may be, it rarely proves fatal. New shoots may show in a matter of weeks, so the only drawback may be a later show of flowers. However, it could well be that your clematis stays dormant for another year – in fact, I have known plants to spring back into life after three years – so do not be in a hurry to dig them out; clematis are notorious survivors!

The only other fungal disease likely to cause any problems is mildew. Some years, there may not be any sign of it in the garden, but when conditions for its increase are suitable it can descend

C. × jackmanii 'Alba'/*Sambucus nigra* 'Purpurea'
The use of a shrub's colouring to enhance a feature of the clematis; in this
instance, the soft mauve shading on the sepals of *C. × jackmanii* 'Alba'.

almost overnight, coating leaves and flowers alike with a fine, milky
veil. Just as some years may bring worse attacks than others, some
areas, and even individual gardens, may be more prone to mildew
than others. In addition, some varieties, i.e. *C. × jackmanii* (and
others in this group) and some of the *texensis* hybrids, are more
likely to be afflicted. As mildew rarely appears before July or
August, these later-flowering plants bear the brunt of the attack –
and at the peak of their flowering season.

If mildew was nothing more than an unsightly, whitish wash,
it might be classed as an 'acceptable' disease. Left unchecked,
however, it can quickly become terribly disfiguring, distorting
leaves and flower buds so much that they fail to open – and those
that do are grotesquely covered in a grey-white powder. There
really is no excuse, however, for reaching the final stage described
above. Unlike wilt, mildew is easily controlled with modern
fungicides. They are readily available, in wettable powder or liquid
form. Those containing triforine or myclobutanil are particularly
effective, and the only proviso that I would make would be to ring
the changes rather than sticking to one particular compound.

Three major pests – slugs, snails and earwigs – attack clematis, but slugs and snails are the most destructive, if only for the reason that they are always with us. They are never going to be eradicated, so the battle becomes more a matter of control. Apart from the obvious signs of slug damage where leaves and young shoots are eaten into (or, in the case of a bad infestation, completely devoured to the extent of leaving only little rounded stumps), it is not often realized that slugs will take the bark from two and three-year-old stems. If it is noticed that more mature stems are taking on a smooth, silver-grey appearance, it is most certainly due to snails – which are even more fond of de-barking. Snails also tend to do more damage to open flowers, probably because they are hiding at that height and, unlike slugs, have not to travel so far. They are particularly troublesome where plants are trained on old stone walls which provide plenty of daytime hiding places. The proprietary products for controlling slugs and snails are so good that they leave no excuse for bemoaning the fact that plants have been eaten away.

Ground bait pellets are no use for old stone walls with copious amounts of mortar missing; the snails that sally forth on nightly forays from these cosy homes are not going to be tempted down to ground level. Instead, spray all over the wall with a proprietary liquid slug killer, and you will be amazed at the number of dead snails, indicating just how many an old wall can harbour! It is particularly important to keep a ring of slug pellets around herbaceous clematis, which have to fight the enemy afresh as the new growth appears every spring.

Earwigs, like slugs, are denizens of the night, usually unseen, only the remains of their nightly feasts greeting us in the morning. Their leftovers seem to cause much deliberation among new gardeners as to what little beast has satisfied its appetite. While earwigs do not kill a plant, or even debilitate a strong grower, it is their liking for the one thing that we have waited all year to see, the flowers, that makes their attentions so devastating. So fond of flowers are earwigs that not only do they reduce fully open blooms to tatters, but they will also bore neat, round holes into the immature flower buds and gain entrance to eat out all the stamens from the inside. The leaves do not escape either, with only the rougher veins remaining. In a dry summer earwigs can be a menace. DDT used to be the surest way of killing them but the nearest alternative now is BHC (HCH) powder, best applied when the foliage is damp with late evening condensation – although it is rather unsightly. My favourite method of earwig control is to roll a 10 in (25cm) wide strip of brown paper into a loose tube and insert it among the stems; these can then be emptied of their contents every couple of days into a bucket of boiling water.

Occasionally, greenfly and blackfly infest the tips of new clematis shoots; they are readily destroyed with any proprietary aphid killer. Mice may, in rare instances, eat both flower buds and swelling growth buds; they are fairly easy to control with poison bait or traps. Bank voles, which have been known to chew the bark from quite large stems at ground level, are not so easy to control. They will not touch the usual poisonous cereal-based baits, and the only method with which I have had any success has been a mouse trap baited with a fresh green pea.

In built-up areas, house sparrows may peck out the flower buds from clematis – as they do with many other plants. If damage is severe or persistent, try spraying with one of the bird repellents.

An explanation, merely, as to why, in some years, *montanas* fail to flower: it is a late spring frost that can kill the tiny, swelling flower buds and there is no defence against such acts of nature.

C. aethusifolia/Rhododendron concatenans
The young buds of the rhododendron echo the stamen colour of the
dainty little flowers of *C. aethusifolia*.

Spring

ABOVE
C. koreana var. *lutea/Rhododendron scintilans*

BACKGROUND
C. alpina/Magnolia stellata

THE PROLIFIC GROWTH, foliage and flower power of a number of spring-flowering clematis species can result in our exercise in compatibility becoming one of slightly distant relationship. Where there is plenty of space in the garden, all the well-known varieties in the lovely family of *C. macropetala* and its cultivars – and similarly the *C. alpina* group – are worthy of a place, with the proviso that strong-growing shrubs are necessary for most of them in order to carry their luxuriance. Unfortunately, in conjunction with increased popularity has come commercialism, which has led to the naming of many (and any) seedlings; some are pretty but many have no greater merit than already existing cultivars, so before buying it is wise to see them in flower unless they bear a name listed by the best-known nurseries.

Their frothy, nodding growth habit looks particularly appealing when peeking through or over wrought ironwork or decorative timber. A 'side-by-side' coming together of the blue and pink shades to be found among these hardy and eager-to-please plants makes for a very pretty effect; and what is wrong with being pretty? Their early arrival, so welcome to us, means less rivalry for their stardom but also that we are restricted to the use, primarily, of evergreen foliage or the bare bones of deciduous shrubs as a foil. *Clematis macropetala* 'Markham's Pink', happily coinciding with the flowers on the laurel *Prunus laurocerasus*, and the dancing charm of *C. alpina* as it weaves through *Magnolia stellata* give an

C. alpina 'Frances Rivis'/*Ilex aquifolium*/ background, *Rhododendron* 'Hawk'
C. alpina 'Frances Rivis' drapes itself over a large supporting holly, while the glorious *Rhododendron* 'Hawk' provides background lighting.

C. alpina 'Columbine'/*Salix lanata*
This early spring clematis announces its arrival before winter's remains have departed and enters into partnership with another herald of the coming season.

C. macropetala 'Snowbird'/*Lithodora* 'Grace Ward'
The clematis pictured in prostrate fashion, with a small but
colourful companion.

inkling of what is achievable, endorsed by *C. alpina* 'Columbine'
scampering through *Salix lanata* – 'lanterns and candles'. The rich,
dark blue of *C. alpina* 'Pamela Jackman' takes to the apple-green
foliage of a bay, *Laurus nobilis*, or perhaps *Abelia* 'Francis Mason';
C. alpina 'Frances Rivis' rests on a sturdy holly with back lighting
provided by *Rhododendron* 'Hawk'. The lovely silver-edged pink
flowers of *C. alpina* 'Jacqueline du Pré' are large for this group and,
although stunning by themselves, can also hold their own given a
suitable host, for example, *Ceanothus prostratus*. A less vigorous
grower is the much sought-after *C. macropetala* 'Snowbird', which
shows off its pristine beauty when adorning such as a small Irish
yew, albeit an association with a time limit. It will just as happily
scramble at your feet, enjoying a little colourful company as
proffered by *Lithodora* 'Grace Ward'.

All the *C. macropetala* and *C. alpina* group are endowed with
the added virtue of succeeding in exposed or shady positions,
where later-flowering cousins would sit and sulk. The Japanese
version of *C. alpina*, *C. ochotensis* – with deep violet or purple
flowers – is no exception and, furthermore, adds shades to the
palette. Their North American relatives again add slightly varying

C. montana 'Wilsonii'/*Picea abies*
This later-flowering member of the *montana* group is seen scaling the
heights to great effect, a task which few can tackle.

shades – *C. columbiana*, with its delicate pale blue, translucent
lanterns, and *C. verticillaris*, reddish-violet – but though desirable,
they are more demanding culturally.

C. koreana has similar pendent flowers and shares the same
dull, purple-red colouring of *C. alpina* 'Ruby'. *C. koreana* var.
lutea, however, opens an entirely new horizon, its soft, primrose-
yellow colour being unique among the spring-flowering clematis
(see page 21). This rare spring colour offers so many exciting
combinations that it is difficult to know which to choose. It does

associate particularly well with the small-leaved, small-flowered rhododendrons in the 'blue' colour range, such as *R. augustinii* and *R. russatum*. It will need a certain amount of annual thinning in order to keep it in check and prevent it from embracing these smaller species too enthusiastically, a treatment which would not be needed with larger growers such as *R.* 'Fastuosum Flora Pleno'. An equally stunning companion to consider is *Salix melanostachys*, with its red and black catkins. These spring-flowering shrubs allow us a 'once-only' display, valued as they are; *C. koreana* var. *lutea*, however, supplements with spasmodic small flushes throughout the season.

Clematis armandii, 'the evergreen one', as it is so commonly called, despite there being other members of the family with this attribute, is a case in point as regards non-compatibility. It is a constant disappointment for prospective purchasers to be told that it will swamp the standard-sized archway in their garden, a fact often not made clear in some magazine articles. It does, however, have the vigour to make its presence felt in an alder *(Alnus glutinosa)* (see pages 28–9). Its large, leathery leaves, shared by the delectable clones 'Snowdrift' and 'Apple Blossom', shout strength – and almost demand the solidity of a wall. The flat surface of a wall also does most justice to *C. cirrhosa* and varieties of *C. cirrhosa* var. *balearica* in showing off the intricate shape of the leaves; the rich green of its foliage and the delicate primrose-coloured flowers are best considered as a backcloth.

Enhancement by proximity is applicable, generally, to the group flowering next in sequence, the *montanas* – their use being, mainly, as a background. They carry their magnificence with such aplomb that, given a wall, fence or pergola of sufficient length and height, the whites and various shades of pink can be grown happily alongside each other. They come into their own, of course, by 'reaching where no other can reach', adding drapery to conifers and a number of other trees which are too greedy of food resources to share with more timorous growers. Conversely, it has to be borne in mind that they will swamp smaller pergolas and archways – and do resist the temptation to clothe the wires of electric and telephone pylons, as they will do it admirably, just to make the removal order more grievous!

Two exceptions to this general zeal are *C. montana* 'Picton's Variety' and *C. chrysocoma*, which are suitable, therefore, to be judiciously used in small town gardens. Scent gives an added dimension; *C. montana* 'Elizabeth', with its vanilla-like fragrance, not only looks delightful growing through a lilac tree but creates a powerful mixing of perfume. The chocolate scent of *C. montana* 'Wilsonii' is not for combining, but is intriguing when within reach – scaling the heights for a sniff is not suggested!

Early
Summer

SCOPE WIDENS CONSIDERABLY when it is time for the large-flowered hybrids to make their appearance, their varying hues ranging from soft to bold and with differing outlines and diameters. Many will suggest combination with others of their own kind, without the need to consider shrubs and small trees as potential partners.

Among the first on the scene are C. 'Moonlight', C. 'Dawn', C. 'Daniel Deronda' and C. 'Miss Bateman'. The unique colouring of *C. koreana* var. *lutea* has been mentioned among the spring-flowering species and C. 'Moonlight' carries this colouring into the large-flowered hybrids; exceptional in itself, it has a most elegant shape. This lovely outline deserves to be shown off to full advantage, so an open shrub or a bare-legged rhododendron is ideal. Its soft colouring can be heightened by a nearby planting such as *Acacia* 'Pravissima', or complemented with foreground colour as provided by hellebores. There are a few other cultivars described as yellow, but 'cream' would be a better description.

It would be hard to flatter verbally the flower of the sturdy C. 'Miss Bateman', white and on the smaller side. It has an attractive dark eye but, surprisingly, its greatest attribute is the green stripe on the sepals. This feature, common to other cultivars – C. 'Barbara Dibley', for instance (on first flowers or by dint of cold spring weather) – is noted with pleasurable surprise or dismay in

C. 'Moonlight'/rhododendron/*Acacia* 'Pravissima' background
A composition featuring this most elegant clematis – and doing justice to the rays of spring sunshine.

C. 'Duchess of Edinburgh'/C. 'Daniel Deronda'
A direct contrast of form and colour, with the use of a double and a
single clematis.

their case, but totally accepted as part of the corsage of the popular
'Miss Bateman'. Just as well to make use of it then, as on pages
40–41, here, where it highlights the more sombre green of the holly
on which it has been placed.

It is surprising how often happy accidents occur; a clematis
can decide on a different route and direction from the one that has
been planned for it, and show superior taste by placing itself next to
a perfect companion. Options in themselves can take some
resolving: for example, to have C. 'Daniel Deronda' and C.
'Duchess of Edinburgh' as a contrast of single cobalt blue and
double-flowered white – or allow the lingering last flowers of
'Daniel Deronda' to provide a magic touch in enhancing the ice-
blue edged sepals of the translucent white double C. 'Chalcedony'?
The two flowering periods afforded by 'Daniel Deronda' – shared
by most of the large-flowered hybrids but particularly generous in
this case – give leeway for a secondary partner or associate. This has
relevance to this particular pairing, C. 'Duchess of Edinburgh'

having only a light second crop. This is, however, again in double form – which is not the case with most other double-flowering clematis, for example *C.* 'Veronica's Choice' and the similarly formed and coloured *C.* 'Louise Rowe'. The early, double flowers can be grown in solitary splendour, or offset by the simple shape of a single clematis, as on page 23, where the plummy-mauve of *C.* 'Kathleen Wheeler' takes up the edging of the sepals on 'Veronica's Choice'. The later, single-flowered form can, conversely, be used to compliment a more blowzy companion.

C. 'Proteus'/*Geranium psilostemon*
A small but colourful plant, lifting and holding its own with a
showy clematis.

That epithet can certainly be ascribed to *C.* 'Proteus', its peony-like flowers being better associated with a foil of simple form and lowly stature. For some reason that can be justified only by experience rather than logic, its flowers look more spectacular viewed from a reasonable distance, late afternoon sun seeming to pick out its 'pinkier' tones. It is a colouring that offers the choice of a totally soft, romantic effect – pulmonaria at its feet perhaps – or the addition of a little spice, which *Geranium psilostemon* does with relish. Its later, single and simplified form can stand eye to eye with a more determinate consort like a foxglove.

With the re-awakening of interest in clematis during the 1950–60 period, there arrived on the scene a few new varieties which caught the public imagination. One of the foremost of these was *C.* 'Vyvyan Pennell'. The rather strange combination of reddish-brown marking on the lavender to violet rosettes is greeted either with enthusiasm or with something rather less, often depending on whether it is the viewer's first acquaintance with a double-flowered clematis. It is not one of the easiest of colours to place successfully, sitting none too happily against brick and looking positively ill at

C. 'Vyvyan Pennell'/*C. uncinata*
Two extremes of shape and size here: 'Vyvyan Pennell' will stand alone in its later, single form.

ease against wooden panelling, but, with a cream or white wall as a backcloth, it takes on an entirely different perspective. It is shown here growing with *C. uncinata*, the latter providing an evergreen surround to an entrance. However, the use of *Anemone × hybrida* 'Monterosa' can greatly benefit the softer hue of the later, single flowers.

Any shrub which is grown primarily for foliage effect is considerably enhanced if the clematis growing with it is either one with a long flowering season or one having two distinct flowering times. Into this category comes *C. × jackmanii* 'Alba' (see page 31),

C. 'Peveril Pearl'/Corylus maxima 'Purpurea'
The deep background of the hazel does justice to the lustrous appeal of
this soft beauty.

which, when given a light pruning, will produce in June a limited quantity of large 'ragamuffin' double flowers that are intriguing, if not to everyone's taste. A much larger slice of the cake is provided by the prolific display of decidedly paler-coloured single flowers, which make their appearance later in the season. If it is wished to settle solely for these, it can be simply achieved by hard pruning in the spring. In general, the milky, translucent or soft colour-infused white appertaining to double-flowered varieties (excepting *C.* 'Duchess of Edinburgh') lends itself more easily to combining with the predominantly blue, pink and lavender shades of the early large-flowered hybrids. When the stronger late summer colourings come along, 'wash-powder white' comes into its own.

There are certain plants grown specifically for the colour of their foliage, whose flowers are virtually non-existent or insignificant, and they are admirable for use as an adjunct or amiable companion. The colouring of their leaves can be highlighted or used as a contrast, be a pallid servant or a lively associate. The word 'plant' is used because, although the great majority are shrubs – particularly the evergreens – there are herbaceous plants grown for their foliage which, by association rather than cohabitation, can be woven into the garden tapestry. Some purple-leaved plants, such as the rather sombre *Prunus cerasifera* 'Nigra' and *P. cerasifera* 'Pissardii', stand as dark sentinels over the entire garden. Livelier purple shading as put forward by the hazel pictured with *C.* 'Peveril Pearl' is attractive and makes far more equable company.

As if to counter the effect of the soft lavender and purple hues most commonly associated with clematis at this season, some of the most vibrant pinks and startlingly vivid carmines come on to the scene. From the soft rosy-mauve with carmine bar of the old favourite *C.* 'Nelly Moser', the slightly deeper *C.* 'Bees Jubilee', the not-to-be-hidden pinks of *C.* 'Lincoln Star' and *C.* 'Scartho Gem', through to the boldness of *C.* 'Dr Ruppel', all these bright colours succumb to sunlight; however, this reaction can be prevented, as they will all perform equally well in shady areas. Vivid colours do need careful placing and are at their best when used to enliven dull, wall-grown shrubs such as *Garrya elliptica*, or the constant unchanging face of ivy.

C. 'Scartho Gem'/variegated ivy
A striking combination, bringing together a flower flushed with 'hot' colouring against a cool-looking host.

Shades of blue fit in almost anywhere – and no other climber can cover the spectrum of this colour with such mass indulgence. The range starts from the satin-textured *C.* 'Mrs P.B. Truax', whose periwinkle-blue flowers are among the earliest to open, through the mid-blue of such as the never-failing *C.* 'H.F. Young', and on to rich, deep blue as displayed by the dependable *C.* 'Lasurstern'. The double-flowered clematis favouring blue make their entrance in early June. A joy among these is *C.* 'Countess of Lovelace', the opulent double blooms heralding early summer, with an equally rewarding display in late summer. So different are these slender, fragile-looking later blooms that any newcomer to clematis could be forgiven for believing that they possess two completely different plants. Not only are the majority of blue varieties found in this season, they also happen to be among some of the most rewarding and easily grown. Apart from the excellent varieties just mentioned, choice alternatives in blue, or bluish, shades which could easily be substituted one for the other in the garden are worth giving space to here. *C.* 'Lady Northcliffe', of a more compact habit, has flowers of such classic outline as to be the very embodiment of how a clematis is imagined to be – with the added virtue of an almost continuous display. Lack of stature is no disadvantage; uses can be found for more compact varieties, such as hiding the bare legs of certain climbing roses, or even of some of their own kind. *C.* 'Elsa Späth', in a deeper shade, on the side of lavender-blue, is a reliable choice and is tall enough at 8 ft (2.4 m) to grow into a cream or yellow climbing rose. The old favourite *C.* 'William Kennett' is one of the most rewarding for the first-time grower. It has the most handsome flowers, with wavy-edged sepals, of the type which perhaps looks inappropriate when in too close contact with other large plants; better hand-in-hand along a wall with similar brethren or as a foil for herbaceous plants. Another most satisfying plant is the so obliging *C.* 'Mrs Cholmondeley', which produces its comely light blue flowers virtually non-stop throughout the summer. Accorded judicious pruning, this variety can be induced to greater height than any of those mentioned above and is constantly recommended for growing in differing aspects. This extended flowering season, combined with taller growth, widens the scope considerably and the pale-blue of its colouring can safely be associated with almost any other colour.

C. 'Beauty of Worcester' is no exception to the rule of the double-flowering varieties commencing their season a week or two later than their single sisters. Its wonderful deep blue colouring is at

C. 'Countess of Lovelace'/*Rosa* 'Bouquet d'Or'
An example of a classic combination, clematis and rose, in its softest form.

49

C. 'Burma Star'/Choisya ternata
The deep, velvet-textured purple of 'Burma Star' is shown off to perfection
when blended into the charms of this popular shrub.

the further end of the blue spectrum. Generous feeding will reward
the grower with a no less spectacular crop of single flowers in late
summer. Another clematis of compact habit, it can decorate
Escallonia 'Peach Blossom' very prettily.

A few shrubs flower spasmodically throughout the season, and
it follows, therefore, that at some point any clematis planted therein
is going to coincide. The Mexican orange blossom, *Choysia ternata*,
always seems to have a few flowers and is one of those shrubs
which can be pruned to whatever height is desired. Its small, starry
white flowers complement the sumptuous velvety texture of the
purple *C.* 'Burma Star', a new variety which flowers over a long
season and whose compact habit means that a position can always
be found for it somewhere, even in the smallest garden.

If large blocks of impact colour are what you desire, the large-
flowered, mid-season hybrids really answer the call. On walls or
fences, the only restriction to combination of colour is the
limitation of one's own imagination. It may be personal choice as to
what is planted where, but there are certain colour combinations
which 'grab by the throat' rather than 'lead by the hand'. Pink

mixed with yellow usually irritates, the purplish-red of the so-called 'red' clematis parked adjacent to scarlet or orange positively screams, and dull or dark purple placed against green foliage just sits unnoticed.

Purists seem to find the idea of large-flowered clematis growing through shrubs incongruous, and yet *C. patens* or *C. lanuginosa* seen scrambling naturally so in the wild would be likely to bring forth gasps of admiration. In the open garden, the mid-season hybrids are probably used to best effect on low to medium-sized shrubs – which themselves have only a short season, and especially so if cut by an early frost – thereby extending what would otherwise be a rather colourless spot. By Nature's design, therefore, the majority of clematis flowers will be combined with leaf colour and texture rather than competitive flower colour.

Two cultivars which flower at this season are pictured here, showing their secondary, late summer flowering. The sensual, soft pink and mauve *C*. 'Mrs Spencer Castle' (see page 119) has equally appealing flowers in both her appearances – the semi-double early ones and the later, less freely dispensed, single ones. *C*. 'Lady Caroline Nevill' is shown (on page 22) growing with a rose in her later guise, as nearly all the early clematis are on the wane before roses have got into their stride. The delicate, blue-tinted, porcelain-like blooms have a timeless, classical beauty which entrances nearly all who first set eyes on them. Although belonging in this season and, indeed, in some years producing an enviable display of semi-double flowers at this time, 'Lady Caroline Nevill' often produces only a scattering – saving all her efforts for the guaranteed late summer crop of single blooms.

C. 'Kiri Te Kanawa' is, deservedly, one of the most popular and most sought-after clematis to have been issued from the Peveril Nursery (see page 116). It stands supreme above other double-flowered clematis, being unique in its unfailing ability to produce such an abundance of double flowers from the current season's growth. The first flowers are borne on side growths from the previous year's stems and may be too full for some tastes, the many sepals packed into a round dahlia-like ball. These earlier flowers have the strongest colour, a rich, deep blue – less intense in later blooms. It is these later flowers which place 'Kiri Te Kanawa' in a class by itself – not quite as double, the cream stamens showing, but produced in large clusters from the current growth in a near never-ending display. (As I write this, in mid-November, a plant outside the window is still producing flowers, albeit of a much paler blue.)

After twenty-five years of hybridizing, during which period I have raised more new quality hybrids than any breeder since the early 1900s, it demonstrates the high esteem with which I regard this new variety that I have, at last, named one after my wife. *C.* 'Patricia Ann Fretwell' (see page 78) is the first pink and red double-flowered clematis raised, its lively flamboyance so distinctive and eye-catching that it attracts even those gardeners for whom double flowers generally have no appeal. An impact seller, and one that I am sure no garden centre would want to be without. A moderately vigorous grower to about 8ft (2.4 m), it has the added bonus of producing a very good show of flower in the late summer and autumn. These later, single blooms do not hold the unique position of the earlier flowers, being pale pink with a deeper central bar, but they do provide late pink colouring which is an added bonus at this late season.

C. × durandii/Rosa 'Buff Beauty'
Still going strong in the cooler days of autumn, *C. × durandii* partners another lovely rose.

OPPOSITE
C. fasciculiflora/Prunus serrula
Delicately pretty flowers and pale, early spring sunshine are set off by the warmth of burnished bark.

Striking-looking clematis such as 'Patricia Ann Fretwell' and 'Kiri Te Kanawa' require more thoughtful planting and, in common with a handful of other cultivars, can be planted in solitary splendour, on a pergola or suitably coated wall, or complemented by the use of softly-coloured foliage or small, hazy types of flowers such as those of myrtle or hebe.

A number of gardeners have a preference for the species and small-flowered clematis, either because they find the larger flowers too gaudy or, more often, because they feel that they fit more easily into semi-natural combinations. By far the greater number of the smaller-flowered clematis choose to flower in late summer and autumn, but there are a few little gems to savour – should you prefer to peer rather than have your attention demanded – which flower towards the end of this mid-season and lead us into the beginning of the next clematis season. However, none among these is suitable for growing through trees and shrubs in the open garden, unless it is of the sheltered courtyard type. Even with the wall protection which is required, it is still prudent to combine them with other climbers or wall shrubs, as their season, though at a useful time, is unfortunately limited to a once-only flowering.

All but two are evergreen, and it is among this selection that some of the most attractive foliage is to be found. From the number of evergreen clematis native to New Zealand, there are three which I have found to be more hardy than the rest of their compatriots. The largest flowers belong to the beautiful *C. indivisa*, which makes for a most impressive display when smothered in hundreds

of 3 in (7.5 cm) pure white blooms – worthy of a sheltered spot on any wall. It is hard to better it when surrounding a frequently used doorway. The richly bright colouring of tulips at its base can enhance and suffice.

Growing, like *C. indivisa*, to 10 ft (3 m) or so, *C. forsteri* has smaller foliage and flowers and requires careful siting. So numerous are the flowers that they almost obscure the foliage and the silky, greenish-yellow colouring calls for close inspection – which affords, at the same time, appreciation of the attractive lemon scent. A softer perfume emanates from the third New Zealand contender, the extraordinary *C. afoliata*, its small, pale yellow flowers hanging from a tangled mass of almost leafless, evergreen stems.

Of the two Chinese species flowering at this time, *C. uncinata* (see page 45) is also scented (to specify is beyond me), its dark

C. tosaensis/Tropaeolum tricolorum
A touch of 'tropical' warmth from the tropaeolum combines with the cool beauty of *C. tosaensis.*

green, leathery leaves creating a foil for its small, white, starry flowers. *C. fasciculiflora* belongs to a tiny select band of clematis which have variegated foliage, and being evergreen as well, it means that we are blessed with year-round attraction (see page 53). The young foliage is reddish with a pink central variegation, changing with age to green with grey variegation. The soft yellow flowers are quite numerous if unscathed by any spring frost to which they are susceptible (they can be out in early April). They are so attractive that the effort of providing cover on frosty nights is well worthwhile.

The two final species are both native to Japan and deciduous. Both will reach a height of approximately 8 ft (2.4 m). *C. japonica,* being a little more twiggy in its habit, produces its small, polished, hanging mahogany bells in twos and threes directly from the leaf axils. *C. tosaensis* is very similar: its leaves are a paler green, but it too has nodding bell-shaped flowers, the colouring in this case a waxy ivory white. Warm, sheltered wall space is always at a premium in any garden but, if full use is made of it, year-round interest can be achieved.

C. japonica and *C. tosaensis* can be used to combine with other early summer-flowering climbers or wall shrubs that require the same favourable conditions, such as the more tender tropaeolums, *Jasminum primulinum* and abutilons. *Rosa banksiae* and its varieties, which flower at the same time, get rather bare around the legs and can benefit from the cosmetic covering of a less vigorous companion. They can also be profitably used to fill the otherwise 'dead' season that precedes the later flowerers such as fremonto-dendron, mutisias and solanum – the last-named, incidentally, making an excellent clematis companion.

At the time when the mid-season clematis start to wane, with just a few stragglers staunchly carrying the flag, there has always been a natural lull in flower production until the appearance of the later, major display. The exact timing of this in-between period is not constant; it is dependent on area and the weather variations between one summer and another but is, normally, from early mid-June until well into July. There will be some precocious flowers from the later performers, but their main show is still some way off.

A few examples, such as C. 'Belle Nantaise' and C. 'W.E. Gladstone', can be obliging, starting to flower in early June and carrying on, but as often as not they tend to miss out on the early crop altogether. In 1956, Percy Picton introduced the now well-known C. 'Hagley Hybrid', which, if lightly pruned, can be relied on to be in flower for early June. After an interval of almost twenty years, C. 'Niobe' was introduced from Poland; this, if given the

C. 'Niobe'/Teucrium fruticans
Shades of red are not the easiest to partner; however, the ruby-red of
'Niobe' is shown off prettily in a silver-green setting.

C. 'Rhapsody'/*Philadelphus coronarius* 'Variegatus'
The sapphire-blue of this sparkling new clematis variety gleams against a
crisply light background.

same treatment as 'Hagley Hybrid', will also help fill this otherwise
rather sparse period. 'Niobe' is a good, easily grown clematis – not
too tall – and a popular cultivar. Its dark red flowers, though not
produced in large numbers at any one time, are constantly repeated
over a very long season. More recently, Jim Fisk introduced *C.*
'Pink Fantasy', which will flower in June, though as its pretty pink
colouring fades considerably in sunlight, it is prudent to plant it in a
north-facing or shady situation. This will, unfortunately, delay
flowering for a couple of weeks, although, once in flower, it does
go on for a long time (see page 1).

As stated in my book *Clematis* (1989), one of the best post-
war introductions, *C.* 'Maureen', appeared rather secretly on the
market without anyone seeming to lay claim to its raising. Since
then, we have been contacted by the son of its raiser, Mr George
Strudwick, who informed us that the gentleman named it after his
granddaughter. This richly coloured, velvety-textured cultivar is a
welcome addition to this in-between period and, although not a
particularly strong grower, it does seem to repeat flower forever –
as the very late blooms show.

Not relishing the prospect of another twenty-year wait, I
decided to try to breed more of these compact, long-flowering
'between-time' plants. Two of these have been named and one is on

general release. *C.* 'Rhapsody' is similar to 'Pink Fantasy' in that a similarly applied light pruning will initiate an early start – with constant flowering through the rest of the season; however, even pruned as category C, this variety is strong enough to be in constant flower and still reach 10ft (3m). There is a scarcity of blue-flowered varieties among the late summer-flowering clematis, which makes the addition of 'Rhapsody' even more desirable. A unique feature in the colouring is that as the deep 'Waterman's ink' blue of the flowers fades, they become even more blue, reversing the pattern of other blue clematis. This colouring makes it an admirable companion for growing with cream and soft yellow variegated shrubs of small to medium size such as *Weigela florida* 'Variegata' and *Philadelphus coronarius* 'Variegatus' (see page 56) – and for climbing roses, of course – but it is particularly suited to shrub roses such as *R.* 'Golden Wings', *R.* 'Nevada' and *R. rugosa* 'Agnes'.

C. 'Maureen'/*Sorbus* 'Joseph Rock'
The plummy richness of *C.* 'Maureen' flowering into late summer, gracing the ornamental sorbus until the tree outgrows its guest.

C. 'Caroline' is a superb clematis, differing from others in this group by virtue of having the ability to flower early, even after being pruned down to 2 ft (60 cm) in the spring. The medium-sized flowers have a nice, crisp outline, progressively produced from near ground level; these are carried over many weeks, making this a spectacular specimen plant for pergola or pillar. The two-tone pink colouring is, again, different from any other clematis, having peach-pink overtones on first opening. Many associations can be found for a warm pink colouring: for instance, highlighting a small purple-leafed hazel or enlivening the darker leaves of *Weigela florida* 'Foliis Purpureis'. A very striking wall combination is formed with *Pittosporum tenuifolium* 'Purpureum'. A universally appealing clematis that brings a warm glow to any garden, it was named after plantswoman Caroline Todhunter, whose own garden gives pleasure and inspiration to many other gardeners.

OPPOSITE
C. 'Caroline'/pillar
The abundant flowering habit of this clematis smothers its portion of archway, with a footing of 'Moses in the bullrushes' (tradescantia).

C. 'Caroline'/Corylus maxima 'Purpurea'
The underside of the hazel's leaves acts as a foil for the soft, warm tones of the pretty clematis 'Caroline'.

High Summer

THE YEAR MOVES into high summer, when the garden incorporates a whole new panoply of shapes, textures and, above all, colour. We welcome red, orange and yellow, the hot colours of summer, which, so fortuitously, are tempered or highlighted, as mood dictates, by the less harsh tones of the almost bewildering range of forms and colours offered by clematis at this season. A range so diverse that, within a span of three months, there is a choice of size from 2 ft (60 cm) border plants to 20 ft (6 m) tree climbers and flower shapes ranging from small bells and stars to the more familiar flat saucers. Above all, though, this is the season that brings roses to the scene, worthy of special mention in the context of being consorts to clematis, the coordination of colours being so ideal and the habitat mutual.

C. 'The President'/*Rosa* 'Mermaid'
Another happy example of togetherness – well-known clematis, popular rose.

OPPOSITE
C. 'Perle d'Azur'/*Rosa* 'Compassion'
This favourite clematis is pictured here as it is so often grown.

Gardeners who are rosarians foremost are likely to consider clematis as filling a subservient role and choose accordingly. Clematis addicts, needless to say, will choose a rose to complement and not overshadow. In truth, a happy marriage is desired on both sides, and adherence to some guidelines can ensure happiness for each camp. It might reassure the real 'rosaholics' who have not recently had the opportunity to visit the Mecca of rose-growing – the Royal National Rose Society's 'Gardens of the Rose' in St Albans – that clematis have been planted there. We were pleased to be invited in 1985 to submit a design plan and supply the required clematis. They now intermingle to great effect with the roses on the main pergolas, and, along with the enjoyment of a visit, lessons can be learned. (A list of roses and accompanying clematis is reproduced on pages 64–5.) The more strongly coloured pairings

ROSES TO PARTNER CLEMATIS	
Roses	Clematis
'American Pillar' (R.) Bright rose-pink with white eye, 10 ft (3 m), July.	× **'Huldine'** Pearl-white flowers, mauve-veined reverse, 10–15 ft (3–4.5 m), July–September.
'Bobby James' (R.) Creamy-white, very vigorous to 25 ft (7.5 m), June.	**'Mme Baron Veillard'** Lilac-pink flowers, pale green stamens, 8–12 ft (2.4–3.6 m), August–October.
'Cécile Brunner' (Cl.) Light pink, 25 ft (7.5 m), June–August.	**texensis 'Gravetye Beauty'** Ruby-red 2 in (5 cm) tulip-shaped flowers, 6–8ft (1.8–2.4m), August–September.
'Claire Jacquier' (Noisette Cl.) Small flowers, yolk-yellow fading to creamy yellow, 25 ft (7.5 m), June–July.	**orientalis 'Bill MacKenzie'** 3 in (7.5 cm) wide pendulous lantern-shape flowers, bright rich yellow, 15–20 ft (4.5–6 m), July–October.
'Climbing Shot Silk' (H.T.) Cerise-pink, shot orange-salmon, June–September.	**viticella 'Minuet'** 2 in (5 cm) white flowers, purple-mauve veined and edged, 10–12 ft (3–3.6 m), July–September.
'Coral Dawn' (Cl.) Coral pink, 10 ft (3 m), June onwards.	**'Peveril Pearl'** Lustrous lilac, violet-tipped cream stamens, 8–10 ft (2.4–3 m), May–June and September.
'Danse de Feu' (Cl.) Orange-red perpetual, 12 ft (3.6 m), June onwards.	**macropetala 'Snowbird'** Pure white 3 in (7.5 cm) wide nodding flowers, 8–10 ft (2.4–3 m), April–May, occasional summer flowers.
'Doctor van Fleet' Soft pink, vigorous to 15 ft (4.5 m), June–July.	**viticella 'Abundance'** 3 in (7.5 cm) pink-red flowers, deeper red vein, 10–12 ft (2.4–3.6 m), July–September.
'Dortmund' (Cl.) Single red with white eye, in clusters, 8 ft (2.4 m), June onwards.	**'Mrs Cholmondeley'** Large light blue with chocolate anthers, 8–12 ft (2.4–3.6 m), May–September.
'Elegance' (Cl.) Large, double bright yellow, vigorous to 15 ft (4.5 m), June–July.	**macropetala** Nodding 3 in (7.5 cm) wide lavender-blue flowers, 8–10 ft (2.4–3 m), April–May.
'Elegance' (see above)	**'Lady Northcliffe'** Lavender-blue, white stamens, 6 ft (1.8 m), June–September.
'Ethel' (R.) Mauve-pink, large clusters, 20 ft (6 m), June.	**'Venosa Violacea'** 4 in (10 cm) purple flowers, overlaid with white veins, 10–12 ft (3–3.6 m), June–September.
'Ethel' (see above)	**'Hagley Hybrid'** Shell-pink, reddish-brown stamens, June–September continuously.
'Francis E. Lester' (H. musk) Single white and pink, 15 ft (4.5 m), June.	**'Comtesse de Bouchaud'** Mauve-pink, 6–8ft (1.8–2.4 m), July–August.
'François Juranville' (R.) Deep salmon-pink, 20 ft (6 m), June–July.	**'Perle d'Azur'** Sky-blue flowers, green stamens, 10–12 ft (3–3.6 m), June–October.
'Guinée' (H.T.) Dark maroon red, 18 ft (5.4 m), June–July.	**'Marie Boisselot'** Large, pure white, cream stamens, 8–12 ft (2.4–3.6 m), June–September.
'Hamburger Phoenix' (Cl.) Rich red, in clusters, dark foliage, 10 ft (3 m), June onwards.	**flammula** Small, starry, white-scented flowers, 10–15 ft (3–4.5m), August–October.

ROSES TO PARTNER CLEMATIS	
Roses	Clematis
'Kew Rambler' Soft pink, deeper edging, grey-green foliage, 15 ft (4.5 m), June.	viticella 'Royal Velours' 2½ in (6 cm) dark velvety purple flowers, 10 ft (3 m), July–September.
'Lady Sylvia' (H.T.) Deep pink, 12 ft (3.6 m), June–September.	'H.F. Young' Large mid-blue flowers, cream stamens, 8–12 ft (2.4–3.6 m), June to September.
'Lady Waterlow' (H.T.) Salmon pink, 12 ft (3.6 m), June–September.	'James Mason' Large-flowered white, dark maroon stamens, 8–12 ft (2.4–3.6 m), May–June and September.
'Lawrence Johnston' (Cl.) Canary yellow, 25 ft (7.5 m), early summer.	'Ascotiensis' Mid-blue, greenish stamens, 8–12ft (2.4–3.6 m), July–September.
'Léontine Gervaise' (R.) Deep salmon-yellow, 10 ft (3 m), June.	'Mrs James Mason' Violet-blue double flowers, single in second crop, 8–10 ft (2.4–3 m), May–June and September.
'Mme Alfred Carrière' (Noisette Cl.) Creamy white, 12 ft (3.6 m), flowers until October.	'Lady Betty Balfour' Bright purple-blue, cream stamens, 8-12ft (2.4-3.6m), September-October.
'Mme Grégoire Staechelin' (H.T.) Rich pink, 20 ft (6 m), June–July.	alpina 'Columbine' Light-blue 3 in (7.5 cm) pendent lantern flowers, April–May.
'Maigold' (Cl.) Deep yellow, 8–12 ft (2.4–3.6 m), early summer, second crop.	× jackmanii 'Superba' Purple, red-barred sepals, June–September continuously.
'Parade' (Cl.) Deep carmine pink, 10 ft (3 m), June onwards.	viticella 'Little Nell' White 2 in (5 cm) flowers, mauve margins, 10–12 ft (3–3.6 m), July–September.
'Parkdirektor Riggers' (Cl.) Bright red, 12 ft (3.6 m), June onwards.	viticella 'Alba Luxurians' White 3 in (7.5 cm) flowers, dark stamens, 10–12 ft (3–3.6 m), July–September.
'Paul Lede' (Cl. H.T.) Pink with apricot shading, scented, 12 ft (3.6 m), June onwards.	'Mme Edouard André' Matt red, free-flowering, 8–12 ft (2.4–3.6 m), June–August.
'Ritter von Barmstede' (Cl.) Deep pink in large clusters, 10 ft (3 m), June–July.	'Victoria' Rose-purple fading to soft heliotrope, 10–12 ft (3–3.6 m), June–September continuously.
'Sander's White' (R) Very vigorous, 18 ft (5.4 m), June–July.	viticella 'Rubra' 2 in (5 cm) bright red flowers, white eye, 10–12 ft (3–3.6 m), July–September.
'Seagull' (R.) Single white, golden stamens, 20 ft (6 m), June–July.	'Gipsy Queen' Rich plummy purple, velvety sheen, 12 ft (3.6 m), July–September.
'Silver Moon' (Cl.) Creamy white, very vigorous, 20–30 ft (6–9 m), June.	viticella 'Purpurea Plena Elegans' double 2 in (5 cm) rose-purple flowers, 10–12 ft (3–3.6 m), July–September.
'The Garland' (H. musk) Blush-white, small daisy-like clusters, 15 ft (4.5 m), June–July.	texensis 'Etoile Rose' 2 in (5 cm) nodding bells, deep cherry pink, silver-pink margin, 8–10 ft (2.4–3.6 m), July–September.
'Wedding Day' (R.) Single white, 20 ft (6 m), June.	viticella 'Mme Julia Correvon' Bright rosy red 4 in (10 cm) flowers, 10 ft (3 m), June–September.
KEY (Cl.) Climber (H.T.) Hybrid tea (H. musk) Hybrid musk (R.) Rambler	

with later-flowering clematis are, perhaps, easier to choose, as instanced by C. 'The President' growing with *Rosa* 'Mermaid'. The rich blue tones of C. 'Elsa Späth' also tone beautifully with this glorious (if brutal) rose. Paler shades ask for more subtle choices, such as C. 'Perle d'Azur' pairing *R.* 'Compassion'. It is an invaluable help, when planning, to have had sight of both rose and clematis, even if the names would seem to indicate their colouring. Even then, observance of this advice doesn't give a guarantee of perfect unison. The rose 'Bouquet d'Or' was planted with C. 'Lady Caroline Nevill' on a pergola in our nursery garden, only to be transposed after its first season – it being decided that its soft tones acted better as a pretty foil for the vibrant C. 'Countess of Lovelace' than *R.* 'Crépuscule', which occupied that spot. The stronger, coppery-salmon tones of this beautiful rose consequently had the gentle-toned, elegant C. 'Lady Caroline Nevill' as its bedmate and they made a happy-looking couple (see page 22).

One group of clematis more than any other engenders surprise, not only for first-time viewers but even among many experienced gardeners, who are unaware of the many delights to be found in it. Until fairly recent times, herbaceous clematis had, generally, been represented in our gardens by only three or four of this large and diverse group; a few others would occasionally make a casual appearance in the catalogues of some alpine plant nurseries. I became so enamoured with these 'Cinderellas' of the clematis world that in the 1960s I started to reintroduce all these long-neglected species. Many of them were no longer in cultivation in this country and, as the collection slowly increased, the fascination that they held for me led me to begin hybridizing among them to further increase the range available.

Not all are easy garden subjects, although some are among the most amenable and it is from the latter group that I have chosen a representative selection to bring to your attention. As a collective group they cover the whole of the summer flowering period, but in order to help in the selection of one particular herbaceous clematis it would seem appropriate to mention them together. One of the first to flower, C. *recta*, has been grown in our gardens since the sixteenth century and varies in height between 3 ft (90 cm) and 6 ft (1.8 m). The amount of flower carried – and, incidentally, the scent – is just as variable, so it is always wise to inquire about the pedigree of any plant you buy. I say this advisedly, as 90 per cent of C. *recta* sold is grown from seed; a poor reflection on many suppliers! C. *recta* 'Peveril' is a fixed clone of shorter stature (approximately 3 ft (90 cm)) and is literally smothered in scented white flowers. The frothy 'white cloud' effect created by a plant in full bloom can be used effectively in the herbaceous border to combine with similarly timed flowers, such as peonies and oriental poppies, or to fill in between the foliage of later summer flowers such as delphiniums and monarda. In the mixed border, planted among shrubs, its floppy growth can be allowed to rest against the shoulder of an uncomplaining neighbour (not on offer among herbaceous partners), some discreet means of support being called for. The season of interest can be extended by the alternative – or additional – use of *C. recta* 'Purpurea', the deep, plum-purple

C. recta 'Peveril'/mixed herbaceous border
This useful and pretty species is pictured here in a typical cottage
garden setting.

young leaves and stems of which make an attractive foil, not only for its own flowers, but as contrast for even earlier companions such as tiarella, primulas and geum.

North America is home to a fascinating group of herbaceous clematis featuring small, nodding, pitcher-shaped flowers; some present a challenge to successful cultivation but not all are so demanding. I cannot resist showing one of these diminutive gems from a family largely populated by more towering relatives.

C. coactilis/Hebe 'Bowles Hybrid'
A contrast in textures: the woolly-coated leaves,
flowers and stems of *C. coactilis* and smooth,
shiny hebe.

C. × *aromatica/Pyrus salicifolia* 'Pendula'
The herbaceous clematis *C.* × *aromatica* laces its way
through a silver-leaved pear, fronting a pond full of
water-lilies and creating a tranquil scene.

C. coactilis is fairly representative of this American group, possessing the typical flower shape and growing to a height of 12–18 in (30–45 cm), but it is distinguished by having the most intriguing covering of soft white down over the leaves, stems and flowers. None of these dwarf 'Americans' have vivid colouring, so the last thing that they require is to have competition from garish companions. A perfect foil is provided by leaf texture such as that of dwarf conifers, the small-leaved hebes, and the foliage or seedheads of earlier-flowered alpines.

A much taller subject, at a height of 4 ft (1.2 m) (if supported vertically), is *C.* × *aromatica*, although it is more likely to be seen lying along the ground or sprawled over whatever happens to be within its range. A plain little flower from its description, but it has the talent to look very pretty grown in this natural way – trouble-free too! The clusters of small, starry flowers are, as the name implies, scented (a soft lemony fragrance); however, unless it is planted on a bank or raised bed, it means paying homage on one's knees in order to enjoy it. Artificial support can be provided by slender shrubby branch growths pushed into the ground around the perimeter or, more naturally, by planting *C.* × *aromatica* under the branches of a small shrub of open habit and allowing it to make its way through. A slender plant, it produces only a small clump of stems, thereby offering the opportunity to try a number of plants in differing situations.

Until fairly recently, *C. fusca* was known in one form only: as a semi-woody climber. In 1981 I received from a Japanese friend some plants of *C. fusca* which he had collected from the mountain area of Hokkaido. These were of a previously unknown variety, which has proved, subsequently, to be a very exciting acquisition. This completely herbaceous clematis which, under more austere conditions in the wild, only reaches a height of 18 in (45 cm), will add several more inches when treated to the richer fare of an English garden. Without support, this means a greater propensity for lying along the ground, which is not necessarily a disadvantage.

This same habit presents no problems at all for *C. gentianoides* (see page 70), for one of the charms of this small Tasmanian species is its naturally prostrate pose. Under favourable conditions these trailing evergreen stems will reach out for 12–18 in (30–45 cm), but in practice it gets severely checked in our winters. Although I have

C. fusca dwarf form/*Anaphalis cinnamomea*
This subtle blend illustrates how even the less obvious clematis can find a suitable companion.

C. gentianoides/at base of conifer
A miniature member of the genus: *C. gentianoides* at the base of a dwarf
conifer, awaiting the arrival of surrounding spring bulbs.

had plants survive for many years in sheltered, well-drained sites, where they associate very well with alpine plants requiring similar conditions, I have now taken to giving them winter protection. In colder areas, the most sensible way to grow them is in pots – to be plunged outside for the summer. Even without a suitable garden, it is worthwhile growing *C. gentianoides* in a pot, if only to confound friends who will not believe it is a clematis!

There is no doubting the hardiness of *C. integrifolia*, for it has long been a firm garden favourite. There are, however, selected forms which are of greater value in the garden than the wild, unadulterated species, these named forms producing more flowers per stem and also having a longer flowering season. Colours range through purple, blue, pink and white, providing scope for many, and varied, combinations. The habit of *C. integrifolia* is to grow to a height of 2 ft 6 in (75 cm) with some support, or, if left to its own devices, to spread along the ground in a cartwheel fashion from the central rootstock with the terminal 12 in (30 cm) or so of flowering stem turning upwards again, creating a circle of flower. If used in mixed herbaceous beds, this natural formation can be used in the front; otherwise, with sympathetic support, the plants can be moved midway to associate with taller subjects. A more informal method which I have found to be very successful, and which allows stems to display themselves at differing heights, is to let them grow through and over small or prostrate shrubs; for example, *C. integrifolia* 'Rosea' is shown here growing through an annually pruned berberis. Many of the smaller hybrid roses make excellent companions, as seen here with *C. integrifolia* 'Pastel Blue'.

C. integrifolia 'Rosea'/*Berberis* 'Roseglow'
Coordination of colour and form between clematis and shrub is illustrated here.

C. integrifolia 'Pastel Blue'/*Rosa* 'Clarissa'
The flowers of the clematis are in their final stages – but leave a legacy of seedheads to dance with this delightful little rose.

71

C. stans is a much stronger individual, able to hold its own against any other plant of equal vigour – although it must not be overshadowed as, in common with all of these herbaceous clematis, it enjoys an open, sunny site. Standing at 3 ft (90 cm) tall, and as much across, it requires as much space as *C. recta*; disparaged as it is by many pundits, however, it might be thought not worthy of such an area. The most important thing is to acquire a good form, not one of the 'off-white' flowering kind most commonly met but one whose tiny, exquisitely shaped flowers are a soft sky-blue – and with a most delicate 'lily-of-the-valley' scent. Admittedly *C. stans* is not for the small garden, but, flowering where space allows, it has a most useful season in September to October and it can provide a light, frothy relief from stronger colours.

C. stans/Anemone × hybrida
A soft and gentle scene, to which *C. stans* contributes, earning it its space in the garden.

C. heracleifolia var. *davidiana*/*Rosa* 'Mrs Oakley Fisher'
A clematis in slightly subordinate role – but in exalted company with this
rose. It is *C. heracleifolia* var. *davidiana*, however, that provides
the perfume.

A more statuesque relative of *C. stans,* having a stiffer, more upright habit, is *C. heracleifolia.* In common with *C. integrifolia,* the type plant itself is seldom grown, being represented in gardens by one of the named forms which, from the gardener's point of view, vary but little between them. *C. heracleifolia* var. *davidiana* is certainly a plant for those whose sense of smell is below par, as, on a warm summer evening, its heavy cloying perfume pervades the surrounding air. For this reason, and the fact that the flowers are better appreciated close up, planting in close proximity to a path or walkway is recommended. The lavender-blue flowers are borne in circular clusters around the stem and are always described as having the appearance of hyacinths, which is, indeed, true. Only slightly less scented, *C. heracleifolia* 'Wyevale' is an extra fine selection, its larger flowers being a rich deep blue. Unfortunately, the curse that afflicts too many clematis, i.e. the use of a popular name for an inferior plant, applies frequently to Wyevale; another form with small, dark blue flowers usually masquerading under false colours! At a height of 3 ft (90 cm) and possessing large leaves, the plant itself is quite striking; it suggests itself for many positions in the garden, although it is wise to choose a background which will advantageously show off the blue of the flowers. The composition of the pathway itself can be considered in this respect, if it is at a level where it will act as the background to the picture, whether in the form of attractively coloured gravel or paving in stone or brick.

If one were to imagine the likely offspring from a marriage between the strong, upright stems of *C. heracleifolia* var. *davidiana* and the mass of vigorous growth with which *C. recta* is endowed, I believe the vision would be one of a bushy, multi-stemmed, free-standing plant of great constitution, covered in beautiful flowers. Alas, the reality is not so in the case of *C.* 'Edward Pritchard'. The beauty of flower is there, certainly, and they are freely produced on each stem, but therein lies the problem: if only more stems of stronger constitution were produced by this plant! It is hardy and not too difficult to grow, but the yearly increase is painfully slow and it is a clematis, therefore, to be planted among companions of equal or less vigour, for if the competition is too fierce, I fear its demise is a certainty. This is, nevertheless, one of those plants that is worth waiting for; its pretty, scented sprays of flower, so light and airy, convey a sense of spring lingering into the heavier days of summer.

C. 'Edward Pritchard'/*Cosmos atrosanguineus*
A coming together of slender stems but with total contrast of colour depth and shape of flower.

Although the stems of C. 'Cascade' grow to a length of between 2 and 3 ft (60–90 cm), they are completely prostrate, and the height from the ground at which the flowers are displayed is dictated by the position and manner in which it is grown. The choices are many and varied: directly on the ground if grown in a raised bed or bank, tumbling over a low wall or stony outcrop on a rockery, or allowed to raise its head and lie over and among nearby small shrubs. The rather tubby, pitcher-shaped flowers, rosy-purple in colour, are, in common with other similarly coloured flowers such as *Lilium martagon*, consigned to a subordinate role if overpowered by strong colours such as the scarlet or orange of poppies. Foliage is, again, the key towards providing a foil; accompanying flowers need to be smaller or of a similar colour tone, for example hebes and heathers. The flowering season is generously long, progressing from June until September and followed, thereafter, by extremely large golden seedheads.

C. 'Cascade'/*Hebe* 'Quicksilver'
One of the smaller clematis gems doing what its name suggests over a rockery face; formative seedheads are already on the scene.

Leaf colour may not, on first consideration, seem to impose the restraints and limitations that the large blocks of primary colours seen in so many flowering plants do, but the wrong choice of clematis with a particular foliage can be as disastrous as choosing a 'wrong' flower combination. It is surprising how one that would seem to be ideal in the mind's eye can, when it reaches fruition, result in the flowers evaporating into thin air. Variegations in cream and green and gold and green, which appear to be obvious choices, are in fact some of the worst offenders in this respect, the light-coloured foliage acting almost as camouflage for pale colours and for some of the small-flowered species. The pinks and warm rosy shades, though, fit in admirably against these creamy backcloths, as do some of the darker blues and purples. There are some excellent cultivars of variegated ivy which, like clematis, are better for not being planted in isolation, as their very permanence can lead to indifference.

The most ardent of clematis fans would be hard pressed to describe favourably the tangled brown mass of winter stems, so it is worth seeking harmonious bedfellows. So called 'blue' and blue-green foliage is predominantly found among the coniferous trees and shrubs and blends easily with any other colouring. Evergreens, and particularly conifers, are used to provide the 'bones' of a garden, either as background or as feature plantings which can, again, by their very permanence, become at times rather dull. The foliage of the clematis chosen for this aspect of 'togetherness' is more important than the colour of the flower; complementing the host foliage is the aim, not obliterating it with a clematis the leaves of which are excessively large or overly abundant. Clematis leaves are predominantly light green to apple-green – the varieties which have rather more than their fair share are better used among shrubs of similar ilk.

We can progress naturally towards the climbers by way of C. × *durandii*, which is, itself, a 'half-way house', being a hybrid between the herbaceous C. *integrifolia* and C. × *jackmanii*. It is, deservedly, a very popular plant, combining as it does the twin virtues of having a long, successional flowering season and sizeable, rich indigo-blue flowers. Although the 4–6 ft (1.2–1.8 m) of non-clinging stems present no problem if they are to be tied in to wires or trellis, a little more thought is required if the best result is to be attained in the open garden. The stems can look very attractive just casually resting on and over dense shrubs or conifers, but unless the garden is very sheltered, the first strong wind is going to blow the stems everywhere. It is far better to provide natural support, allowing the plants to grow through a spaced framework, as provided by those staunch clematis allies, shrub roses.

C. × *durandii* was introduced in 1870 and for 120 years it was the lone example of a C. *integrifolia* crossed with a large-flowered hybrid. In 1990 we marketed a new C. *integrifolia* hybrid, which, in the space of just four years, has achieved a popularity that has surpassed expectation. The neatly shaped 3 in (7.5 cm) flowers of C. 'Arabella' are smaller than those of C. × *durandii* and are produced in far greater number (see page 25). On a young plant the individual flowers do not look particularly outstanding, but the mass effect of the combined rosy-purple, red-flushed, newly opened flowers mixed with the mauve-blue older blooms creates an ever-changing curtain of colour and form. It has the distinction of being probably the longest-flowering clematis with which to adorn

C. × durandii/ Rosa 'Leda'
This most popular semi-herbaceous clematis enjoys bright summer sunlight with the shorter-seasoned rose.

a garden, coming into flower in June, reaching a peak through the next three months and then slowly waning in October. It is an ideal clematis for a small garden, growing to only about 6 ft (1.8m) in height. As with other non-clinging climbers, an open framework shrub rose makes an ideal companion – and the mixture of warm purple to blue shading, plus its striking cream stamens, provides a multiplicity of colour choices. These could include the unusual lilac shade of *Rosa* 'Cymbeline', the flesh-pink flowers of *R.* 'Shropshire Lass', through deeper pink tones and even into the range of the yellow-leaved shrub *Choisya* 'Sundance'.

As we reach July the memory of all those spring *montanas* seems far away, yet there is still one *montana* which leaves those cooler days and frosty nights to its more precocious relatives. *Clematis montana* 'Peveril' (page 12) brings its flowers to us at a useful time, as the majority of the white-flowered species are still a few weeks off. Its pretty outline and long, shimmering stamens really entitle it to be grown where its flowers can be seen individually. Another plus factor of this variety is that it has a less vigorous habit than most other *montana* varieties, a feature which means that it is not, therefore, precluded from small gardens. Even so, all the *montana* groups make a lot of growth, and any companion planting, unless it is of equal vigour, is better placed on the periphery, as the most well-intentioned of embraces can soon lead to suffocation. This does not exclude every shrub from being used as a host; there are many of strong constitution, such as hollies and lilacs, which are willing to stand a fair amount of competition.

The 'large-flowered' hybrids which flower in late summer and autumn are thus described to differentiate between these and the smaller-flowered kind which predominate at this season. Compared to the large flowers displayed by their earlier-flowering relations, this is something of a misnomer, and 'medium-flowered' would be a more appropriate description. *C.* 'Ascotiensis', however, is rather an exception; its flowers have a more pointed outline and larger size that set it apart from others flowering at this season (see page 81). Until quite recently, it also shared the distinction of being one of only two 'blue' clematis flowering at this time – an uncontested attribute held for 100 years. A plant of easy disposition, it is suitable for many situations provided that competition is not too intense. An extra feature which never seems to receive recognition is the strong violet scent which is wafted from it on warm, humid days.

C. 'Patricia Ann Fretwell'/*Pittosporum* 'Irene Paterson'
Only undemanding company tolerated here – and in subsidiary role at that!

C. 'Gipsy Queen'/Eccremocarpus scaber
The orange and red shades of the intriguing *Eccremocarpus scaber* will
also pair happily with the splendid C. 'Gipsy Queen'.

C. 'Gipsy Queen' is an archetypal clematis, with its rounded,
deep purple flowers produced in one glorious surge of colour. A
long-time favourite for generations of gardeners, its vigorous, free-
flowering habit provides cover for walls, arches, pergolas and small,
easy-going trees, as represented by apple and pear. Great swathes
of purple in isolation can become overpowering after a while. A
comrade designated to lift the unrelieved heaviness can be lively, as
in the case of *Eccremocarpus scaber,* or a subject that is pale or
perhaps unimpressive when alone – in which case it can, in return,
receive an injection of vitality and warmth. Candidates could
include the white-flowered everlasting pea *Lathyrus latifolius*
'Albus', a pale-toned honeysuckle, *Lonicera japonica,* or another
clematis, *C. campaniflora*.

OPPOSITE
C. 'Ascotiensis'/trunk of *Chamaecyparis* 'Erecta'/*Malvastrum lateritium*
'Ascotiensis' decorates a tree trunk, with *Malvastrum lateritium*
constituting a further attraction as well as providing shade for the
clematis roots.

Whereas the strong constitution of *C.* 'Gipsy Queen' would automatically ensure its inclusion on any list of varieties recommended as suitable for newcomers to clematis growing, it is certainly not a quality which could be applied to *C. florida* 'Alba Plena' and *C. florida* 'Sieboldii'. Not easy clematis to grow successfully, certainly, but the fact that they are not hardy should not allow them to be dismissed. Both these varieties have a universal appeal – 'Alba Plena' with its white, green-flushed pompons, and the stunning, purple-centred white flowers of 'Sieboldii' – and the following may help to avoid the frustration of vendor and customer in having to inquire and diagnose whether growing conditions are suitable for this not easily suited duo.

C. 'Perle d'Azur'/*C.* 'Continuity' through apple tree
An unexpected combination. *C.* 'Perle d'Azur' arrives to meet up with a *montana* – in July.

OPPOSITE
C. florida 'Alba Plena'/in container on patio
A stunning species shown as a patio specimen, accompanied by other plants contributing their varied colourings.

Frost-tenderness alone certainly excludes them from cold, northerly climes, and generally, unless a warm, sheltered corner with well-drained soil can be provided, it has to be a choice between permanent conservatory cultivation or pot-grown culture with shelter provided for winter protection. It makes an excellent pot-grown specimen, and can be used to great effect among differing, similarly pot-grown subjects. Although not pictured, *C. florida* 'Sieboldii' is more generally available than 'Alba Plena' and therefore better known; as one variety is merely a sport of the other, similar cultural needs apply.

One of the most popular clematis ever raised – and well past its 100th birthday – *C.* 'Perle d'Azur' still habitually figures among the top ten best-sellers. One reason, undoubtedly, lies in competition

C. × eriostemon 'Hendersonii'/*Rosa* 'Buff Beauty'/*Galactites tomentosa*
A happy co-existence of herbaceous clematis and shrub rose, backed by
the architectural foliage of macleaya with *Galactites tomentosa* adding its
own touch of colour.

being severely restricted, there having been only one other late-flowering blue clematis, but it still deserves its accolade judged on its merits. Of true × *jackmanii* persuasion, its medium-sized mid-blue flowers, bountifully produced over many weeks, associate so well with climbing roses (see page 63) that it is rarely seen growing any other way. However, with a lighter than normal pruning, this strong-growing cultivar can be happily induced to climb into small trees (see page 83), where it can mingle with berries or the flowers of other climbers. Whereas, at a height of between 10 and 15 ft (3–4.5 m), 'Perle d'Azur' may be a little too tall for a small garden, the newer cultivar C. 'Prince Charles', although not as blue in colour, is more compact and, therefore, more suitable for a limited space.

C. × *eriostemon* 'Hendersonii' holds the unique position of being the first recorded cross between two clematis species. Introduced in 1835, it may appear to be a little antiquated now, but this is still a desirable cultivar and it has certainly lost nothing in vigour since its inception. Not too tall at 6–8 ft (1.8–2.4 m) and providing hundreds of flowers over a long period, it does, however, produce a large number of stems, which may preclude its use where space is limited. The deep purple-blue colouring is enhanced dramatically if a brighter, more lively colour is used as a highlight;

small amounts are more effective, and one spike of verbascum or a small clump of rudbeckia or heleniums can be sufficient. If it is to be used in conjunction with a medium-sized shrub, in order to provide support and contrast in colour, it is wise to wait until the intended host is sufficiently large before the clematis is planted.

The original crossing of *C. integrifolia* and *C. viticella* – which gave rise to *C.* × *eriostemon* – has, over the years, been repeated on a number of occasions, although none of the results has been sufficiently distinctive to warrant a separate identity. Such an easy and eager-to-please plant deserves more colour and variations. The culmination of many years of trials and tribulation has produced, here at Peveril Nursery, a new colour break which, it is hoped, will be felt to be well worth the 150-year wait. It would be too dogmatic to say that this colour is an improvement on the original, as colour choice is always a very personal judgement, but it would be hard to deny that it creates more impact in a garden setting. *C.* × *eriostemon* 'Heather Herschell' not only possesses all the attributes of *C.* × *eriostemon* 'Hendersonii', but the satin texture of the 2 in (5 cm)

C. × *eriostemon* 'Heather Herschell'/*Salix exigua*
The silky sheen of this exciting new clematis cultivar is shown fronting a silver waterfall of willow.

nodding bells seems to be even more pronounced in its shading of soft to deep pink. With a little forethought, clematis flowers of any size can be successfully woven into the garden fabric – but one has to rejoice at the ease with which small flowers such as those of 'Heather Herschell' fit so naturally into their chosen position.

Too well known to need either a description or a recommendation, the only advice offered in respect of *C. × jackmanii,* and the superior form *C. × jackmanii* 'Superba', is to be more adventurous in its positioning as opposed to its usual obligatory station surrounding the doorway. As is also the case with *C.* 'Gipsy Queen', rich purple can be imposing in some situations but in others it can appear almost oppressive without a lively, or

C. × jackmanii 'Superba'/*Sorbus aucuparia* 'Kirston Pink'.
The warmth of late summer sun plays on the purple of this well-known clematis and its host.

OPPOSITE
C. fargesii var. *soulei*/*Potentilla* 'Gibson's Scarlet' at base of apple tree
The delightful pure white flowers of *C. fargesii* var. *soulei* lower themselves from the tree branches to meet the clear red of the potentilla.

lightening, foil. 'Gipsy Queen' is pictured on page 80 with *Eccremocarpus scaber;* however, the same, or similar, choices can be successfully used for both *C. × jackmanii* 'Superba' and 'Gipsy Queen' when the latter is taking its curtain call. Members of the same family can fit the bill admirably, examples being *C.* 'Hagley Hybrid', *C.* 'Comtesse de Bouchaud', *C. viticella* 'Margot Koster' and *C. viticella* 'Abundance'.

Cast in a similar *C. × jackmanii* mould, *C.* 'Star of India' is far more effective when planted in isolation than any of its monotone purple relations, the plum-red bar along its sepals creating a more lively-looking flower. This is especially so when placed against soft grey limestone or light painted walls. Light green foliage (pages 60–61) can also provide an effective background.

C. fargesii has a 'wilding' look about it; even when transposed into the artificial confines of an English garden, it still manages to

convey a sense of its natural Chinese environs. This can be a rather vigorous climber and severe pruning will be needed, if the preference is to use it as a wall plant, in order to keep it to an allocated space. It can be given more freedom if allowed to scramble through a medium-sized tree (see page 87), and as white-flowered climbers are none too common in the earlier months of summer it can be effectively used to enliven dark conifers or gloomy yews. The 1½ in (4 cm) wild-rose blooms will spangle the branches over many weeks; although never giving a mass display, there always seem to be scattered sprays. These little white flowers which stare cheekily back at the spectator can stand the impundence of *Potentilla* 'Gibson's Scarlet' at their base.

Bright 'buttercup' yellow is not a colour that immediately springs to mind when considering clematis, but *C. orientalis* and its near relatives all possess flowers of varying shades of yellow. Although quite a large family botanically, from a garden point of view there is little to choose between the majority of them – and two, or possibly three, would suffice for even a large garden. In the bright yellow range, *C. orientalis* is as good as any, provided a

C. orientalis 'L & S 13342'/*Ilex aquifolium*
The silver seedheads take their turn to gleam against the holly as the
yellow-gold flowers take their curtain call.

C. texensis/Plumbago capensis
Two choice plants, chosen as conservatory
companions.

C. texensis × *C. versicolor* hybrid/*Convolvulus cneorum*
Clematis and convolvulus sharing each other's
company – and their mutual need for a sheltered spot.

good clone can be found. It should be safe to buy one of the named forms, but so many of these are being grown from seed nowadays that even more confusion is being added to an already chaotic situation. *C. orientalis* 'Bill Mackenzie' has the largest flowers, approximately 3 in (7.5 cm), of a very bright yellow (and a long season covering from late June until October) and followed by silvery seedheads, which last remarkably well through the winter storms. A plant of 'Bill Mackenzie' growing over a rather rough hawthorn hedge on former premises created about 20 ft (6 m) of billowing waves of gold and silver, becoming a yearly focus of admiration. At present we have another plant which grows approximately 25 ft (7.5 m) up a large Lawson cypress. Not quite as vigorous, *C. orientalis* 'L & S 13342' has delightful, finely-cut foliage with thick-sepalled flowers in a softer ochre yellow.

One small, select group may truly be described as the aristocrats of the clematis world. Consisting of only six cultivars, the *C. texensis* hybrids are among some of the brightest gems with which we can bedeck our gardens and, despite their exotic appearance, no other clematis look more natural scrambling over low shrubs. *C. texensis* is the only scarlet-coloured species in this vast family, and although it has passed on its many virtues to its hybrid offspring it is, itself, barely hardy enough to be grown outdoors in Britain. It does, however, make a fine conservatory climber, the neat, glaucous foliage providing an attractive foil for other plants even when not in flower. Its main contributions to the garden are its splendid hybrids, the sheer brilliance and vivacity of which enliven any position. Fortunately, the difficulties of successfully growing *C. texensis* have not been passed down to these hybrids – all have proved to be of easy disposition and, oddly enough, they will withstand more extreme soil conditions than many of the more commonly grown varieties.

C. texensis 'Duchess of Albany' is the cultivar most commonly offered for sale, its clear, soft pink colouring easily distinguishing it from the other, more red-toned cultivars. All the *C. texensis* hybrids are strong, vigorous growers to approximately 8 ft (2.4 m):

C. texensis 'Duchess of Albany'/*C. viticella* 'Venosa Violacea'
A variation in shape between these two clematis, but colouring
that is compatible.

C. texensis 'Sir Trevor Lawrence'/*Erica vulgaris* 'Gold Haze'
Starring even from ankle height, illustrating the scope for growing the
desirable *texensis* hybrids.

'Duchess of Albany' probably heads the list for vigour, so much so, that in some seasons it will throw 10 ft (3m) long leafy shoots without any sign of flower. Why it should do this in some gardens, in some years, is something of a mystery, as none of the other *texensis* hybrids suffer from this problem. A proviso in this respect is that they are not planted in the shade; an open, sunny position is the one essential pertaining to all in this group to ensure flowering.

From the original *texensis* crosses which were named by George Jackman in 1890, only two remain with us to the present day – *C. texensis* 'Duchess of Albany' and *C. texensis* 'Sir Trevor Lawrence'. When one sees the stunning effects created by a gentle overlay of bright carmine, tulip-shaped flowers which so dramatically transform the most dreary shrub, it seems incomprehensible that they never really captured the public imagination at that time. Twenty years ago, 'Sir Trevor Lawrence' (see page 18) was rescued from the edge of extinction; happily, it is, today, once more established in many gardens. This is even more surprising when one considers that not only is 'Sir Trevor Lawrence' free-flowering but it manages to be so over a period of four months, considerably widening the choice for combination with other plants, both in and out of flower. All these upward-facing flowers are best planted below eye-level to obtain maximum effect, as the most intense colour is concentrated in the interior. The thick, fleshy flowers seem particularly palatable to slugs and snails and, although these will not be much of a problem on prickly or thorny shrubs, they will definitely have to be controlled if the clematis is grown on the ground or nearly so, for example over heathers, which associate so well with any of the *texensis* hybrids.

Most shrubs tend to have a rather brief flowering period – sometimes extended by colourful fruits – which calls for rather precise timing if it is wished to combine the flowering times of both host and companion. This exercise can be helped immensely if the clematis used has a long flowering season. It is not a problem which arises when roses are used in the supportive role, as the long flowering season ensures that, at some point at least, both will coincide. When both have long flowering seasons, as do the rose and *C. texensis* 'Gravetye Beauty' shown growing together, a long and interesting combination is easily achieved. The deep, ruby-red colouring of 'Gravetye Beauty', although rich, does really need a lighter background to accentuate this richness. Whereas the distinctive tulip-shaped flowers of the other *texensis* hybrids are maintained almost to the end, those of this cultivar expand rather quickly into an open star shape; this is considered by some to be a defect, but they do combine happily with small, solid-looking flowers such as those of species roses, choisya, or the even smaller blooms of pernettya and heathers.

All these survivors date from around 1900, and the last of these 'Golden Oldies' is no exception; in fact, it came near to disappearing along with *C. texensis* 'Sir Trevor Lawrence'. By virtue of having a large percentage of *C. viticella* in its parentage, *C. texensis* 'Etoile Rose' is markedly different from all the rest of this group. It has lost the upturned flowers which so easily distinguish the others, and its nodding flowers are seen to better advantage if it is planted as an upright climber rather than as a scrambler, the majority of the flowers being above eye-level. This is not difficult to achieve, as the extra vigour obtained from *C. viticella* means that even though it annually dies to ground level, 10 ft (3 m) of regrowth is normal, and the main requirement is to ensure that the supportive feature is tall enough. The fact that it has a flowering season extending from late June/early July until October gives almost unlimited scope for many and varied plantings.

These bright colours perhaps do not harmonize quite as well with roses (unless chosen with very great care) as do most of the other clematis, but some enjoyable companions are to be found

C. texensis 'Gravetye Beauty'/*Rosa* 'Ballerina'
An example of a shrub rose ideal for playing host to this group
of clematis.

among other climbers and shrubs. A memory that lingers is of a large shrub of *Buddleia alternifolia,* the weeping habit and soft lavender flowers of which were completely interwoven with the nodding cherry-pink bells of *C. texensis* 'Etoile Rose'. One of the main causes of failure when first attempting companion planting is using either a shrub or a climber which is so dominating, both at the roots and in top growth, that the poor clematis is never going to have a chance. In some instances, however, a little 'cheating' can bring about a result which, at first sight, would seem impossible. Here 'Etoile Rose' is shown intermingled with the soft yellow leaves of the golden-leaved hop, which when grown in the open

C. texensis 'Etoile Rose'/*Humulus lupulus aureus*
A means to an end! The hop is pot-grown in order to curb its growth in line with its exalted company.

OPPOSITE
C. texensis 'The Princess of Wales'/
C. 'Mme Grangé'
Texensis as grown against a wall – one rich colour matched with another.

garden makes so much growth that little else has any chance of competing. However, with the clematis happily enjoying the freedom of open ground planting, and the hop restricted to the confines of a pot, a happy compromise is achieved.

There are a number of reasons why no *texensis* hybrids have been raised since the early 1900s, the principal one being the sheer level of skill required actually to hybridize with *C. texensis.* The first hurdle is to acquire and grow *C. texensis* itself. It had always been my ambition to produce more of these brightly coloured, hardy climbers and, after many setbacks and disappointments, we released and named in 1984 the first two new *texensis* hybrids in eighty years. The one which we had the honour to be allowed to name after HRH The Princess of Wales has exceeded all expectations and is widely acknowledged as the clematis that one must have – resulting in almost a cult following. It was recently voted the finest new clematis raised and, in the short span of one decade, it is now to be found growing in almost all the temperate countries around the globe.

C. aethusifolia/Rhododendron concatenans
The colour theme of the clematis and the rhododendron shown on page 33
is continued in their seedheads.

C. texensis 'The Princess of Wales' has the most vivid colouring of any clematis hybrid, the deep, vibrant pink having a luminous quality to be seen rather than described. The plant itself is strong-growing and has the added bonus of an even longer than usual flowering season – very often commencing in late June and continuing on until cut back by frost. It can be used as a wall climber, as shown, or planted to grow over shrubs or roses (see page 19). *Magnolia soulangeana* is a magnificent sight in spring and is often planted as a centrepiece. Unfortunately, after flowering, this once splendid centre of attraction becomes a rather drab, green mound throughout the summer. One such magnolia, seen in a friend's garden in July, was planted with *C. texensis* 'The Princess of Wales', which covered one side of the tree with literally hundreds of flowers, transforming what would have been an otherwise 'dead' spot into an awe-inspiring sight.

C. texensis 'Ladybird Johnson' has smaller, dark red flowers which are purple-toned around the edges of the sepals, and is an equally strong grower. A warm, sunny placement is absolutely essential, as this variety does not really get into its stride before August or September – but it is most useful for providing a late red colour in an otherwise waning season. It is worth mentioning, while on the subject of *C. texensis* and its hybrids, that although clematis wilt (see the chapter on diseases and pests, page 29) is rarely a problem, they are in varying degrees prone to mildew.

C. × triternata 'Rubro-marginata'/*Eucalyptus pauciflora*
The clematis adds a dainty tracery to the sickle-shaped leaves
of the eucalyptus.

'Ladybird Johnson' and 'Étoile Rose' are the worst affected, while 'The Princess of Wales' can often escape competely. I am always at a loss to understand why some gardeners will watch a plant become crippled by mildew when a cure is so easily applied by spraying with a fungicide at the first signs of disease. To be forewarned is to be forearmed.

There are a small number of clematis (and, incidentally, shrubs also) whose flowers are too delicate in colour or form to vie with other larger or more colourful flowers. This is not to imply that any of these are insignificant, merely than an appreciation of texture or delicacy of colour is lost if competition is forced upon them. Examples of these really come into their own when it is wished to add interest to a shrub whose own splendour is but a memory. *C. aethusifolia* is a very slender, short-growing climber. If used as a companion to a shrub, it requires one which grows to no more than 3–4 ft (1–1.2 m), as this is a clematis which will not thrive given too much competition. It is better to plant this species in close proximity to a walkway, not only to observe the dainty little ½ in (1 cm) bells (see page 33) and delicate, parsley-like foliage, but to be able to take full advantage of the light 'lemon' scent.

Another clematis which is best planted in an easily accessible position is *C. × triternata* 'Rubro-marginata', not only in order to take advantage of the hawthorn scent which pervades the area in close proximity, but also to appreciate the colour of the flowers.

On close examination, there is a definite partition between the purplish-red and the white marking on the sepals but, from a distance, this same colouring appears to form a camouflage and can easily escape attention, even when smothered in bloom. At 15–20 ft (4.5–6 cm), this is a moderately tall grower and as it is usually seen flowering at its ultimate height, its defects are compounded. A simple solution, to create a more pleasing effect, is to use a support, be it post, pergola or tree, of no greater height than 8–10 ft (2.4–3 m), allowing the final few feet of flowering shoots to fall back on themselves in a tumbling cascade of bloom. If desired, the effect can be heightened by the addition of a second clematis from the range of larger-flowered cultivars, as shown.

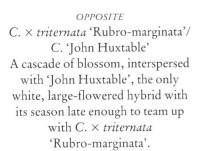

C. 'Venosa Violacea'/*Lonicera nitida* 'Baggesen's Gold'
'Venosa Violacea' shows itself to be at home with shades of yellow.

OPPOSITE
C. × *triternata* 'Rubro-marginata'/ C. 'John Huxtable'
A cascade of blossom, interspersed with 'John Huxtable', the only white, large-flowered hybrid with its season late enough to team up with C. × *triternata* 'Rubro-marginata'.

A number of shrubs which are grown entirely for the colour of their foliage can provide some of the most attractive backgrounds for clematis flowers. Although almost any clematis can be used on one shrub or another, the object is to enhance the colour of the host and not obliterate it with clematis foliage. Shrubs of a uniform colour lose little from having a goodly portion of their area obscured; variegated ones have more to offer of themselves and, for these, choosing a clematis with small or fine foliage is as important as the colouring of the flower. C. 'Venosa Violacea' has foliage which never seems to intrude wherever it is placed and, fortunately, a colouring which blends happily with a varied number of plants. The purple and white-veined flowers, which are so distinctive, combine well with most roses as well as with a large number of other clematis. As it grows to a height of around 6–10 ft (1.8–3 m), it can adequately mantle a medium-sized shrub.

C. akebioides/Lonicera nitida
C. akebioides is seen here in its later stages, with the seedheads adding
their own softening touch.

C. fusca, already described in its newly discovered dwarf form (page 69), has similarly coloured flowers in its more commonly met climbing form. Intriguing, rather than colourful, these intensely woolly little flowers always attract attention, providing a talking point even among non-gardeners. It is another clematis which is better planted without immediate competition, the flowers better for being highlighted by herbaceous plants with complementary-coloured flowers sited in the foreground. This also allows a few of the clematis stems to be recumbent along the ground rather than being tied back to the wall.

Although it will reach a height of 10 ft (3m) or so if grown vertically, *C. akebioides* looks far more interesting if grown as it is naturally in the wild – scrambling over scrub and low shrubs. It is another clematis which has more than a single interest to offer, the attractive, neat, blue-green foliage and fluffy, platinum-coloured seedheads providing additional interest following the flowers. These are not over-exciting but are pretty in a quiet way, the soft yellow having a shiny, satin-like appearance and, when subjected to full sun, taking on a dark red flush along the outer side of the sepals. Many gardens contain the more commonly grown spring-flowering shrubs such as forsythia and flowering currant, which, after a welcome early show, leave nothing but a ten-month wait until the cycle is completed again. A clematis such as *C. akebioides*, scrambling over them, can easily add another four or five months of interest, allowing for both flowers and seedheads.

Modern houses tend to have smaller gardens, often to the extent of having no garden as such, only a small, paved area, and the need has arisen for smaller, more compact plants which will grow in a small patio bed or in containers. Various dwarf and compact-growing plants have been bred to cater for this expanding market (as, witness, the phenomenal increase in 'patio' roses). Many clematis can, of course, be grown in containers, but they are still climbers and require a tall framework for support. The Japanese grow these pot-grown plants over small balloon-shaped bamboo frames and although the end result is attractive it is all very time-consuming. It had, for a considerable time, been one of my aims to breed a new clematis to fill the gap in this new environment.

C. fusca/Lamium aureum/
Malva sylvestris just visible
Although this is the climbing form of *C. fusca,* it is pictured in recumbent fashion in sympathy with the fallen stem of the mallow.

C. 'Lord Herschell'/*Elymus glaucus*
A portrait of contrasting colour
and form: pot-grown foliage is
placed behind the container in
which C. 'Lord Herschell'
is nurtured.

C. 'Mme Edouard André'/
C. *flammula*
The frothy effect of C. *flammula*
softens this direct
contrast of colour and form.

C. 'Lord Herschell' can best be described as a new concept in clematis; one which could be adequately termed a 'patio clematis'. The multiple stems form a bushy plant to a height of only 1½–2 ft (45–60 cm); however, compactness alone is not a sufficient attribute in itself and any plant in a small area must earn its keep. 'Lord Herschell' does this admirably, by constantly producing flowers for many weeks through the summer and into autumn. The flowers themselves are similar in shape to the ever-popular *texensis* hybrids and possess a velvety texture to their rich purple colouring. If grown in a container, complementary schemes are limited only by the number of other container-grown plants which can be accommodated in the space available. Other uses can be found for such a pleasing little plant, for instance, in small beds and borders or for draping the top of a low retaining wall – which it could share with other low-growing plants.

Colour of flower is, undoubtedly, the prime consideration when choosing any plant, but the attraction of perfume also rates highly with many gardeners. Unfortunately, very few clematis are blessed with the added allure of scent and, of those which are, only a small percentage are climbers. A few of those which have a perfume can hold their own with any exotic competitor – and are as well known for their distinctive and varied scents as for their flowers. The *C. montana* group includes scents of vanilla, cedarwood and chocolate; *C. rehderiana* possesses a renowned aroma of cowslips and *C. flammula* a fragrance redolent of sweet hawthorn, which seems to typify balmy summer evenings.

This attribute apart, *C. flammula* can be a spectacular sight with its small, white, starry flowers borne *en masse* into large, billowing white clouds. One of the attractions of white flowers is their ability to associate with most other colours, and many attractive combinations can be achieved using the light, frothy effect of this particular species to counterbalance the heaviness or brightness of larger-sized flowers. *C.* 'Mme Edouard André' is just one example of the type of harmony which is possible, and a very good clematis itself wherever grown – one of those plants with a *raison d'être* of aiming to please, an easy cultivar which achieves a pleasing balance of growth, foliage and flower.

There is no reason why planting has to be restricted only to pairs, and a three-dimensional effect can be brought into being by the addition of a herbaceous clematis to accompany two climbers; *C. integrifolia* 'Hendersonii', for instance, could front those just mentioned. *C. integrifolia* 'Olgae' or *C. integrifolia* 'Pastel Pink' would be candidates should *C. flammula* be partnering, say, *C. viticella* 'Abundance', *C.* 'Comtesse de Bouchaud' or *C. viticella* 'Margot Koster'. *C. campaniflora*, with its long, slender stems and tiny bell flowers of blue-white, can provide a backcloth to the richness of such as *C.* × *jackmanii* 'Superba' or *C. viticella* 'Abundance' – with *C. integrifolia* 'Tapestry' or *C. heracleifolia* var. *davidiana* completing the picture.

C. × *jouiniana* 'Praecox', with its soft grey-blue panicles, can also provide a backdrop if grown in upward mode as an alternative to heaping over a tree-stump or softening a low wall. It needs pruning to form a framework instead of being cut to ground level, and has the restriction, perhaps, of blue as its climbing companion. This is to allow for the autumn tints with which the foliage of *C.* × *jouiniana* 'Praecox' is endowed, extending to red-orange tinges in the generally yellow tones. The restriction to blue comes down to large-flowered hybrids which produce good second crops, as is the case with *C.* 'Lady Northcliffe' and *C.* 'The President' or, for certainty, *C.* × *durandii* and my own cultivar, *C.* 'Rhapsody', which comes into its own. *C. integrifolia* 'Pastel Blue' could well complete this picture.

Some clematis, no matter how pretty, seem to be denied general recognition because of not quite reaching the ideals set by the rest of the genus. Today, more than ever before, plants are demanded which flower for the longest possible length of time. This is understandable if the garden is very small, but it does mean that plants such as *C. serratifolia*, the flowering season of which lasts for only four to six weeks, do tend to be ignored. The flowers, which have a similar shape to the spring-flowering *C. alpina*, are a clear primrose-yellow with contrasting purple stamens; delicately pretty, and even the foliage is an attractive, light, fresh green. After flowering, silky seedheads add extra interest for a few more weeks and, if some lonely shrub can be found to let this clematis scramble over, it will more than justify its keep.

It would be an impossible task to have to say that any one particular variety was the most highly favoured from among such a large and varied genus; however, I must admit to holding a special affection for *C.* 'Victoria'. For a plant which has been in existence since 1870, it never seems to have the full recognition bestowed on the similar flowering *C.* × *jackmanii* and *C.* 'Perle d'Azur'. Indeed, it has many similarities to the ever-popular 'Perle d'Azur' – the growth habit, freedom of flowering and flower shape – only the colouring being different. In a newly opened flower, the colour is deep, rosy-purple – more rosy along the midrib – and it gradually ages to soft heliotrope. It is when the plant is displaying flowers

C. serratifolia/*Cotinus* 'Grace'

The gentle, primrose-coloured flowers of *C. serratifolia* are pictured in a serene pondside setting with amicable companions.

through varying degrees of colour change that it is at its most charming. The warm purple colouring combined with the massed flowering is eyecatching, even from a distance, and creates many possibilities for pleasing combinations or even for highlighting the last remaining flowers on many of the now departing roses and other climbers. One of the most popular of climbing roses, *R.* 'New Dawn', is of such a delicate shade of pink that it almost requests a companion that is sufficiently deep and warm-toned without being overpowering; one need look no further than *C.* 'Victoria' for this and any other rose of similar hue, such as *R.* 'Ophelia'. Any gardener lucky enough to have a tall shrub of *Abelia grandiflora* can have a similarly matched free-standing combination.

C. 'Victoria'/*Sorbus cashmiriana*
Retaining its vivacity to the end, 'Victoria' prepares to take her 'curtain call' and allow *Sorbus cashmiriana* to take the stage.

OPPOSITE
C. viticella/*Rosa* 'Zéphirine Drouhin'
The quiet demeanour of *C. viticella* contributes a restraining richness to the voluptuous vanity of *R.* 'Zéphirine Drouhin'.

The majority of all the previously mentioned clematis, from spring through to autumn, may be happily deployed in the open garden, i.e. climbing over naturally supportive trees and shrubs. However, one group of clematis above all others are so perfectly suited to fulfil this role that, once discovered, no tree in the garden will remain unadorned. *C. viticella* and the small-flowering hybrids derived from this species are some of the most easily grown clematis, rarely, if ever, suffering from clematis wilt. Growing to a height of between 10 and 20 ft (3–6 m), they are eminently suited for the majority of large shrubs and small garden trees. *C. viticella* has been grown in this country since the mid-sixteenth century and is still a garden-worthy plant. The deep purple colouring does require careful placing, and the alliance of a livelier, or even vivid, colour is a virtual necessity. As shown, it contributes a restraining richness to the voluptuous vanity of *Rosa* 'Zéphirine Drouhin'. If the chosen position does not lend itself to a bright colour, then a more gentle combination can be achieved by planting the softer mauve-pink and off-white *C.* × 'Pagoda' to cover the lower half of *C. viticella*.

The debt owed to the greatest of clematis hybridizers, Francisque Morel, becomes even more apparent when it is realized that, of the limited range of *viticella* hybrids available, the majority were bred by him at the turn of the century. *C. viticella* 'Abundance' is one of these and its more open, saucer-shaped

flowers and slightly less nodding habit than that of the wild species, typify the greater number of the following hybrids. *C. viticella* has bequeathed not only the pretty nodding habit – so desirable in flowers which reach above eye-level – but also the asset of producing hundreds of flowers over a very long season, i.e. July to October. The red colouring of any flower is none too easily combined with flowers of another hue, and the pink-red of *C. viticella* 'Abundance' is no exception, enhancement by foliage and by any flowering plant placed in the lower foreground being the easier option. Silver-green and blue-green foliage create a perfect foil, and *Cedrus atlantica* 'Glauca' will give many years of pleasure before this eventually large tree outgrows its companion. The many silver-blue cultivars of *Chamaecyparis lawsoniana*, for example 'Fletcheri', have foliage which is too tight or forever moving and which clematis seem unable to grasp. As some of these trees become more mature, they also become more openly branched and then the possibility arises of adding a climber as company.

A white clematis is a white clematis – and it may appear difficult to become enraptured by any particular one. *C. viticella* 'Alba Luxurians', however, is a beguiling little clematis which holds a strange fascination for most who set eyes on it. It is not starkly white but an almost 'see-through' opaque white, each sepal terminating in a bright green tip which blends in well with softer shadings. A large shrub of *Buddleia davidii* in any of the lavender shades, the soft-hued foliage and flowers of *Rosa rubrifolia* or the leaf colour of a large *Cotinus* 'Foliis Purpureis' can be mirrored in the similarly coloured stamens of this clematis. If grown on a wall or small tree, the same stamen colouring could be accentuated by the use of another clematis, such as *C. viticella* 'Purpurea Plena Elegans'.

C. viticella 'Alba Luxurians'/*Buddleia davidii*
This much-loved cultivar weaves its capricious way through the branches of its host.

It is not surprising, when one considers the colour of *C. viticella*, that most of the hybrid progeny are garbed in some shade of purple. A lot of named hybrids which were in varied shades of purple and on offer 100 years ago have long departed the scene, and from reading descriptions of them it is clear that they would not have made the grade today. One purple clematis that has survived is *C. viticella* 'Etoile Violette', due in part, I believe, to the attractive, moderately large boss of creamy-yellow stamens enlivening the matt-surfaced purple. It is also one of the most free-flowering of any hybrid and has larger flowers at 3–4 in (7.5–10 cm) than most in this group; even so, the colour is such that it needs, more than any other hybrid, some intimately combined colour designed to lift and lighten. Any of the yellow climbing roses, such as 'Maigold', 'Golden Showers' (page 13) or 'Dreaming Spires', will reflect the stamen colour, or, if it is wished to grow it through a tree, the bright yellow fruits of *Malus* 'Golden Hornet' can look most striking. The berries of *Hippophae rhamnoides* will perform the same function; the silvery foliage is, itself, an attractive foil even without fruit. Another hybrid having similar larger flowers coupled with the same free-flowering attribute, *C. viticella* 'Margot Koster', can look very effective grown singly or, perhaps, combined with *C. flammula*, on a pole or arch – its deep, rosy-pink colour fronted by a clump of *Eryngium alpinum*.

The one other *viticella* hybrid sporting larger flowers, *C. viticella* 'Mme Julia Correvon', is, without doubt, one of the most effective clematis. Its bright rosy-red colouring stays an effective shade until sepal fall and without fading to the beetroot shade which bedevils many other reds. The large, creamy-yellow stamens form an added contrast in a clematis which no beginner should be without. This very easy and free-flowering variety starts flowering earlier than most other *viticellas,* often in the second half of June, and continues into August and September. As mentioned earlier, 'reds' are not the easiest of colours to mingle and seem more comfortable occupying their own space, either in a small tree (page 14) or on a wrought iron pergola, fronted by herbaceous plants in silver or white such as *Artemisia lactiflora* – playing it safe perhaps!

The same choices could be used to equal effect if the bright crimson of *C. viticella* 'Rubra' were used, but here, the smaller 2 in (5 cm) wide flowers have a closer affinity with *C. viticella.* These smaller flowers look more at home climbing over a common green holly or bright green conifer and, with the ability to climb several feet higher than *C.* 'Mme Julia Correvon', are more competent for these situations. The text may appear to suggest that only the availability of a natural support gives the opportunity for growing the *viticellas* – however, all of them are equally suited for covering large walls and this, of course, provides opportunities for additional and more varied combinations. *Hydrangea petiolaris*, often grown on a house wall, can be used as support for *C. viticella* 'Rubra', thereby adding a new colour dimension to a plant rather jaded at that time of year. If in more adventurous mood, try 'Rubra' intertwining among the green, pink and cream leaves of *Actinidia kolomikta*.

Even more suited to a white wall are the deep, reddish-purple flowers of *C. viticella* 'Royal Velours'. Imaginative interplanting is demanded if the rich velvet sumptuousness of this aptly named cultivar is to be utilized. On a white wall its sultry splendour would suffice unfettered, but adjacent to dark stone or free-standing greenery it needs lifting by being silhouetted against *C. flammula*, perhaps – or boldly contrasted with the lively orange of *Eccremocarpus scaber*. If grown through a wall-trained pyracantha, the sharpness of the orange berries would serve equally well. When grown through a small flowering crab, the dark waterfall of blossom as it cascades from the tips of the branches can create a most striking union. Try *Malus floribunda* with its small red and yellow fruits, or the more striking *Malus* 'Veitch's Scarlet' with its large, bright red fruit. If preference veers towards the softer tones, try a planting of 'Royal Velours' with the gentle, creamy tones of *Lonicera japonica* 'Halliana'.

The white, rose-purple shaded flowers of *C. viticella* 'Minuet' are colourful enough to be grown in isolation though an apple or other fruit tree, but can also create a striking scene if grown through one of the ornamental crabs. *Malus* 'Echtermeyer', with its reddish purple fruits, has a nice weeping habit which allows a more cascading effect; *Malus* 'Wisley' has similar dark fruit and bronze foliage. On a wall or pergola, almost any rose can look comfortable with 'Minuet', be it the dark red of *Rosa* 'Ena Harkness' or, for a completely different impression, the burnt orange of *Rosa* 'Climbing Bettina'. *Clematis viticella* 'Little Nell', on the other hand, looks positively lonely if not grown in company. Pretty if seen at close quarters, the rather wan flowers, white with pale mauve-pink edges, demand a more strongly coloured companion to draw the eye and raise appreciation of the subtle attractions of 'Little Nell'. *Clematis* × *jackmanii* grows to a similar height, and the merging of the small and larger flowers looks appealing; in general, this allotted task of acting as a foil is one that it performs admirably.

C. viticella 'Royal Velours'/*C.* 'Mme Baron Veillard'/*Prunus serrula*
The velvet-rich flowers of *C. viticella* 'Royal Velours' among a medley of companion plants, including the rosy-lilac *C.* 'Mme Baron Veillard' and the striking blue spikes of *Salvia uliginosa*.

C. × 'Huldine'/*C. viticella* 'Purpurea Plena Elegans'
The combining of two clematis of equal vigour, the colouring of
C. viticella 'Purpurea Plena Elegans' accentuating the central bars of
C. × 'Huldine'.

For quite a percentage of gardeners there is no attraction to be found in any kind of flowers which are double in form. However, some who have no liking for this feature in the large-flowered clematis are still fascinated by the neat, double rosettes of the two examples in the species. One of the more commonly seen of the *viticella* group, *C. viticella* 'Purpurea Plena Elegans' is appreciated not only for its miniature chrysanthemum-like blooms but also for its tenacious capacity for growth and its mass flowering in conditions which some clematis would find untenable. The soft rosy-purple colouring is pleasingly bright and commands attention whether it is grown alone, or with the intention of either being subordinate to or dominating some other colour. This ease of growth and tolerant colouring suggests many and varied mixes and the following suggestions will, I hope pave the way. At this time of year, the ever popular *Buddleia davidii* has to be one option; the common soft lavender form will look anything but common when in unison. If room is available for that vigorous, soft lilac-pink rose 'Paul's Himalayan Musk', then, given a lighter than normal pruning, 'Purpurea Plena Elegans' will be competitively placed to intermingle. If space is lacking for such an exuberant display and is restricted to, say, 10 ft (3 m) or so, try the equally pale rose 'Ash Wednesday'.

All the *viticellas* mentioned are at, or near, their 100th birthday; compared to *C. viticella* 'Mary Rose', however, they are but mere infants. The fascinating and rather lengthy account of how this 'thought to be extinct' *C. viticella* sport was rediscovered has been published on numerous occasions. To précis the background to it: in 1981 I discovered this plant growing on the wall of a Devon mansion, and research verified it as being a survivor of the 'double purple Virgin's bower' described by Parkinson in 1629, making this the oldest known clematis cultivar. As would be imagined, any plant which has survived for over 350 years has to be a strong and vigorous grower and, rightly enough, in suitable growing conditions it is capable of achieving 20 ft (6 m). This clematis – the only other double-flowered *viticella* – has slightly smaller, spiky pompons of a most unusual smoky-amethyst shade.

C. viticella 'Mary Rose'/*C. viticella* 'Little Nell'
Draping a small damson tree, two of the more reticent clematis
co-exist happily.

It is a colour that definitely needs careful placing and, if demurely elusive in the shade, a dramatic change ensues when pierced by sunlight. Therefore, although a sunny position is essential, it is prudent to provide for sunless days by way of a light background or interplanting with highlighting climbers. Colours that can only be described as 'in between' can be induced to favour in one way or the other dependent on the companion chosen. As an illustration of this, the colouring of *C. viticella* 'Mary Rose' comes across as more of a warm purple if grown through the creamy-yellow, lavender-tinged flowers of *Buddleia weyeriana* 'Moonlight' – whereas, if

C. viticella 'Brocade'/*Pyrus salicifolia* 'Pendula'
A vibrantly exciting new cultivar displayed against a willow-leaved pear.

backed by a pink wall or entwined with a similarly coloured rose like *Rosa* 'Complicata', the blue tones in its flowers are emphasized.

The final three *C. viticella* hybrids are the result of ongoing work at Peveril Nursery, to extend the range of this obliging and versatile group. *C. viticella* 'Elvan' is one of the more vigorous hybrids; its 2 in (5 cm) flowers are of a more nodding habit than most – and, in its three-month flowering period, it will present literally hundreds of soft, warm-purple flowers, each having a feathered creamy-white central band (see page 11). The soft purple shades common to many clematis are so easily accommodated when it comes to pairing that it would be hard to create a *faux pas*. Among schemes which look particularly effective with 'Elvan' are the use of bright pinks, as with *Rosa* 'Bantry Bay' and *R.* 'Parade', and, in complete contrast, the muted deep yellow of *Buddleia weyeriana* 'Golden Glow', bringing about a pretty effect. Two of the most commonly planted yellow-leaved trees, *Robinia* 'Frisia' and *Gleditsia* 'Sunburst', also form most attractive pairings.

C. viticella 'Tango' is a brighter version of *C. viticella* 'Minuet', with a red-toned coloration to the smaller, more rounded blooms. Such jolly flowers can brightly clothe a fruiting pear, damson or similarly colourless tree. All the *viticellas* require their rather bare legs to be disguised; in the case of 'Tango', clumps of the white-flowered *Achillea ptarmica* 'Perry's White' or any similar perennial will fulfil this task, including one of my favourites, the ever-flowering *Tradescantia* 'Innocence'.

The newest addition, *C. viticella* 'Brocade', although possessing the free-flowering attributes common to this family, is noticeably different. The shape of the flower is more akin to the spring-flowering *C. montana*, but it is the light-red colour which makes this cultivar so distinctive. The mauve overtones which are consistently apparent in all the 'red' clematis, particularly as they fade, are absent in 'Brocade', giving an initially brighter colour and, also, a cleaner rose-pink as the flower prepares to leave. So new is this variety that only the minimum of combinations have been tried and, as with any bright colour, discretion being the best option, reliable pairings have been sought. Silver-grey is certainly a safe foil for the reds but, if a tree such as the popular *Pyrus salicifolia* 'Pendula' is used, it has to be remembered that in fifteen years or so the host will have outgrown its guest. The same criterion would apply to the equally silver *Pyrus canescens,* but it does provide a chance to ring the changes! *Pyrus elaeagrifolia*, however, can be kept to a large shrub more easily, and the silvery-leaved *Salix exigua* and *Salix elaeagnos* can be pruned regularly to any suitable size. If planted against a wall, a fronting of Miss Wilmott's Ghost, *Eryngium giganteum,* would fill the bill admirably.

An ever-increasing number of gardeners are finding fascination in the less flamboyant, small-flowered varieties of clematis. *C.* 'Peveril Peach' and 'Peveril Pendant' were both raised in order to extend the rather limited range. *C.* 'Peveril Peach' has 1 in (2.5 cm) long urn-shaped flowers with the tips of the sepals curling back; the clear pink colour extends to both surfaces, with definite peach-pink overtones on the inside. Complementing this colour are the attractive blue-green leaves, and coupled with a long flowering season, it makes for an attractive pot-grown specimen. Growing to a height of around 6 ft (1.8 m), a wall-trained shrub of the chaenomeles family would prove an ideal partner, so providing a

C. 'Peveril Pendant'/*Euonymus* 'Emerald 'n' Gold'
The bell-shaped flowers of the clematis dance delightfully on the euonymus, to which they add a new dimension.

OPPOSITE
C. 'Kiri Te Kanawa'/pergola
A diva! Only a prop is necessary – no supporting cast required.

continuity of flower. Should a more direct contrast be desired, this could be a similarly wall-trained autumn-flowering ceanothus (preferably in soft-blue tones, for example 'Gloire de Versailles') – and a pretty picture they would paint.

At a slightly taller 8 ft (2.4 m), *C.* 'Peveril Pendant' has slightly larger, nodding, bell-shaped flowers. Enjoying an equally long flowering season, the reddish-purple colouring does require more thoughtful placing. There will still be sufficient of the late, pale pink flowers of an escallonia to provide a light contrast in colour; however, on a closely pruned wall-trained shrub these flowers would be disposed in a more concentrated manner than scattered around one which is free-standing. The same criterion would apply to *Ceanothus* 'Perle Rose', except that more of its flowers should be naturally harmonizing in the flowering season of *C.* 'Peveril Pendant'.

C. thibetana/ Leycesteria formosa
A companion chosen to highlight the colouring on the reverse of the sepals
of *C. thibetana*.

Very few clematis have foliage which is capable of providing a focal point on its own merit. *C. thibetana*, however, has exceptional ferny leaves, further enhanced by the beautiful glaucous (blue-grey) colouring. The flowers are not particularly eye-catching and are best appreciated at touching distance; even so, the lime-green yellow colour is interesting and will appeal to anyone fascinated by the unusual. Grown on a wall this variety is capable of covering a 10 ft (3 m) square, but grown as a scrambler, a medium-sized shrub would suffice to curb its vigour. As the flowers are not usually abundant before late summer, it is all the more easily accommodated among the reddish and generally warmer tones which abound at this time of the year.

I feel sure that *C. viorna* has evolved with the specific intention of proving that a plant has to have neither large nor colourful flowers in order to demand attention. A written description – 1 in (2.5 cm), reddish-purple shading to creamy-yellow, urn-shaped, nodding flowers – would hardly seem to set the pulses racing. It is a fact, nevertheless, that when our own plant is in flower it never fails to attract – even when more flamboyant relatives are nearby. The seedheads are almost as striking as the flowers, being inordinately large for the size of the flower. Growing through a wall-trained escallonia, the flowers of *C. viorna* take over as the escallonia finishes its main flush and also complement the later blooms of another of my favourite clematis, *C.* 'Mrs Spencer Castle'.

118

There is no distinct cut-off between seasons, and even the timing of these is controlled by the vagaries of our climate. Equally, with clematis, a variety with a normally recognized flowering season can drift, or, occasionally sail boldly, into the adjoining season. Some, like C. × 'Huldine', never seem to know quite when to start; in some years it can be as early as July, in others not until late August. Whenever it decides to start flowering, you can be certain of a continous curtain of bloom until stopped by winter's frosts. This most endearing of clematis is at its prettiest when viewed from below, with the light filtering through the opalescent sepals creating the impression of a pale mauve-pink bar along each one. As long as the host or wall is tall enough, this is not a difficult picture to achieve, as C. × 'Huldine' is a vigorous plant, reaching 10–15 ft (3–4.5 m) in a season and almost the same in width. Although it is an easy and vigorous cultivar, this distinctive and charming clematis must be grown in full sun to give its best. Not many other clematis have sufficient vigour to cope with its embrace – and the only practical companions have to be chosen from among the more vigorous *C. viticella* hybrids (see page 112).

C. 'Mrs Spencer Castle'/*C. viorna*
An illustration of how two totally different clematis can come together
in harmony.

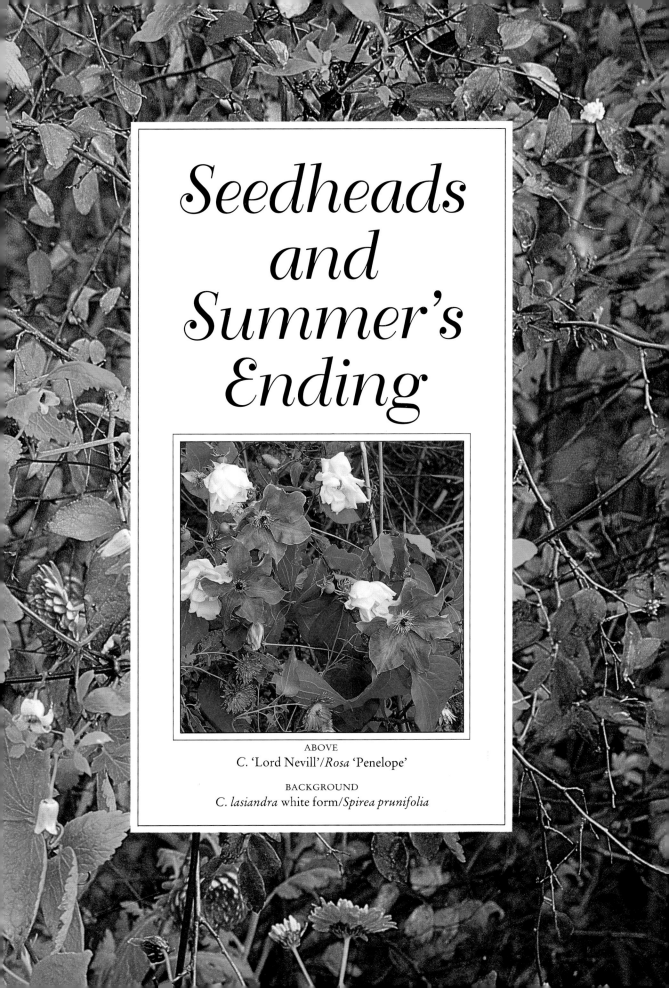

Seedheads and Summer's Ending

*A*s SUMMER SLIDES inexorably into autumn, clematis colour is provided in many different ways. For some clematis this late season is their natural flowering time; in addition, very many of the summer-time flowerers will carry spasmodic crops of bloom until stopped by frost. The value of seedheads should not be underestimated – they really come into their own as flower colour diminishes.

There are only two large-flowered hybrids which truly belong to this late season; others are merely interlopers lingering on from earlier glories. Both of these flower over approximately the same period, starting around the beginning of September and going on well into October. In our garden, *C.* 'Lady Betty Balfour' (see page 3) is usually the first to start, and what other plant could give such a tremendous display of purple-blue at this time of year? Fortuitiously, both these late-flowering cultivars are of strong constitution and easily accommodated, the only extra requirement being a sunny position, a condition which is applicable to all these late-flowering varieties. *C.* 'Mme Baron Veillard' is equally free-flowering and, although the rosy-lilac colouring is not exactly stunning, the flower does possess a mellow beauty in keeping with the season – indeed, the last belle to leave the ball.

As we approach the end of the gardening year, it becomes admittedly more difficult to match flower to flower, and any pre-arranged plan can be assured only if foliage or berries (assuming a fruitful year) enter the equation. *C. tangutica* could just as easily

C. tangutica/ Lilium lancifolium
Spectacular seedheads, such a feature of *C. tangutica*, take over to act as a foil to the exuberance of the lilies.

C. 'Mme Baron Veillard'/*Chamaecyparis* 'Squarrosa Sulphurea'
Foliage tones with the stamens of this hybrid.

have fitted into the summer section along with the closely related *C. orientalis*, but it was photographed in September – the last few flowers remaining to salute the silvery seedheads for which this species is so well known. They will still provide a point of interest right through until March, when spring gales finally dissipate them. Not all seedheads survive the winter in the manner of *C. tangutica*, but many more do provide added interest long after the flowers are gone. The red-tinged seeds of *C. aethusifolia* (page 96) are particularly handsome; a few others of particular note include the red and green clusters of *C. viticella* 'Minuet', the large spheres of soft gold of *C.* 'Daniel Deronda' and, though not as long lived, the silvery plumes of *C. flammula* and the *alpina* and *macropetala* group.

It almost seems incongruous that, as the majority of plants are winding down ready for winter, there are some for which this late season means an awakening. *C. connata* is one of these, rarely starting to flower before the beginning of September and all but gone in the space of four weeks. Within those weeks, however, many hundreds of primrose-yellow bells will have opened and fallen, dispersing a soft lemon scent in the meantime (see page 124). Desirable as this species is, it is not a plant for the small garden as its very vigour necessitates a fair amount of space – reaching, as it does, to 20 ft (6 m) annually. It can be used in solitary splendour on a pole or wall, or as a backing for late border plants, but there are many mature, medium-sized acers and cherries which could well do with some embellishment. *C. terniflora* is almost as vigorous and is, in essence, a larger form of the better known *C. flammula*. When grown in warmer climes than ours it possesses an almost overpowering fragrance, dispensed less freely in our cooler, autumn air. If room can be found for another vigorous grower, then this species can be quite rewarding, with its multitude of starry flowers. Our own plant regularly covers a rather scruffy old hazel hedge and, as a pair of goldfinches annually nest in it, what better reason for leaving it there?

C. lasiandra (pages 120–21) requires rather more sun than the average British summer gives and for this reason it sometimes fails to get into its stride before the frosts cut it short. *C. lasiandra* itself is a rather dull purple colour, so it is far better to opt for the white-flowered form (actually white with a delicate pink basal stain); if it gets into its stride, it is a most endearing little plant. On a warm, sunny wall, flowering is no problem, but it comes into competition with many worthwhile plants queueing for this choice position. Another clematis fighting for this sunny wall space is *C. pierrottii* (page 125), offering just about the final display of the year and still flowering well after the first frosts of winter. Although not an evergreen species, the exceptionally bright, fresh green foliage

C. connata/Sorbus aucuparia
A mixing of citrus shades – contrasting berries
and bells.

C. apiifolia/Rosa rugosa 'Frau Dagmar Hartopp'
Autumn foliage echoed by *Chrysanthemum*
'Emperor of China' in the foreground.

retains its verdure until well into the winter. Unlike some of the autumn flowerers, it is not overpowering and an annual pruning will keep it to a 6 ft (1.8 m) square space. It can usefully highlight the berries of a wall-trained firethorn or cotoneaster.

In some years, many of the summer-flowering hybrids will reward with a third, light crop of flower in the autumn. This cannot, of course, be assured – and is to be appreciated as a bonus, especially as the same circumstances have the equivalent effect on many of the roses. A wet summer, followed by a drier autumn, appears to expedite this situation and, even though autumn colours may be less rich, these unplanned, late combinations are all the more satisfying for their spontaneity. The following examples were photographed at the end of October and, although those such as *C.* 'Lord Nevill' are an unexpected pleasure, there are a few stalwarts that can be fairly relied upon to have a final fling before winter.

C. 'The President' (see page 62) has for long been a favourite, mainly on account of its long flowering season. *C.* 'Niobe' (see page 55) is a mere stripling compared to the last named, yet is almost as well known, not only for its dark ruby colouring but, again, for its extended flowering period. *C.* 'Lady Northcliffe' is hardly ever without its mid-blue flowers between June and winter, and on one memorable occasion even managed a resurgence at Christmas. The ever-popular, ever-satisfying *C.* 'Mrs Cholmondeley', with its taller habit and lighter blue flowers, can usually be relied upon to be carrying at least a few flowers.

The colouring of the leaves in autumn is not one of the factors normally considered when choosing a clematis. Indeed, the one detrimental feature about them is the manner in which they resolutely hang onto their long dead foliage throughout the winter. A small number, however, can usually be relied upon to depart with a cordial flourish. This tends, mostly, to be towards the golden shades – or yellow in the case of all the herbaceous *C. heracleifolia* group, an added attraction with these being the scent of new-mown hay detectable as the foliage dies. *C.* × *jouiniana* var. 'Praecox' can also normally be relied on to assume a golden hue but can, if weather conditions are right, be shaded in soft pink or purplish tones. Most members of the *C. montana* group change to varying shades of purple, being particularly notable in *C. chrysocoma* with the addition of coppery tints. This renders it almost as striking as the warm bronze of *C. apiifolia*, shortly following the departure of its starry white flowers.

And so, with the onset of winter, comes a brief and well-earned respite for this unstinting genus. It is hoped that, from within these pages, enthusiasm has been imparted to engender even greater enjoyment from cultivation of the clematis.

C. 'Lord Nevill'/*Rosa* 'Penelope'
Late October, and the final fling for both clematis and rose: lacking their full colour, but staying long enough to greet *Chrysanthemum* 'Paul Boissier'.

C. pierrottii/pyracantha
Stretching the season to its end, just one step in front of 'Jack Frost', the clematis is shown to advantage against the bright red berries of the pyracantha.

Species Hardiness Zones

The clematis species listed here may be considered winter-hardy in the zones indicated.

Zone	Winter temperature	
	° Fahrenheit	° Celsius
1	below −50	below −45
2	−50 to −40	−45 to −40
3	−40 to −30	−40 to −34
4	−30 to −20	−34 to −29
5	−20 to −10	−29 to −23
6	−10 to 0	−23 to −18
7	0 to 10	−18 to −12
8	10 to 20	−12 to −7
9	20 to 30	−7 to −1
10	30 to 40	−1 to 4
11	above 40	above 4

C. akebioides – zones 6–9

C. aethusifolia – zones 6–8

C. alpina – zones 5–9

C. apiifolia – zones 6–9

C. armandii – zones 7–9

C. coactilis – zones 6–8

C. connata – zones 6–9

C. fargesii var. *soulei* – zones 6–9

C. fasciculiflora – zone 8

C. flammula – zones 6–9

C. florida – zones 6–8

C. fusca – zones 6–9

C. gentianoides – zones 7–9

C. heracleifolia – zones 4–9

C. indivisa (C. paniculata) – zones 4–9

C. integrifolia – zones 4–9

C. x jackmanii – zone 4

C. koreana – zone 6

C. koreana var. *lutea* – zone 6

C. lasiandra – zones 6–9

C. macropetala – zones 6–9

C. montana – zones 6–9

C. orientalis – zones 4–9

C. pierrottii – zones 6–8

C. recta – zones 3–9

C. serratifolia – zones 6–8

C. stans – zone 5

C. tangutica – zones 4–8

C. terniflora (C. maximowicziana) – zones 4–9

C. thibetana – zones 5–8

C. tosaensis – zones 6–9

C. texensis – zones 5–8

C. uncinata – zones 8–9

C. viticella – zones 4–8

C. viorna – zones 5–8

Index